# Becoming What We Are

# Becoming What We Are

Classical and Christian Readings of Modernity

Jude P. Dougherty

Edited by Catherine Dougherty

The Catholic University of America Press
Washington, D.C.

Compilation, preface, and new text copyright © 2024
See the Acknowledgments for a listing of chapters previously
published.

The Catholic University of America Press
All rights reserved

Cataloging-in-Publication Data is available from the
Library of Congress

ISBN: 978-0-8132-3661-2
eISBN: 978-0-8132-3662-9

*For*
*William Frank*

# Contents

| | | |
|---|---|---|
| Preface | | ix |
| Acknowledgments | | xi |
| Introduction | | 1 |

### Part I

| | | |
|---|---|---|
| 1 | Becoming What We Are | 11 |
| 2 | Durkheim at the Founding of Social Science | 15 |
| 3 | Cicero | 23 |
| 4 | Larry Siedentop | 27 |
| 5 | Washington's Solemn Contemplation | 33 |
| 6 | Charles de Gaulle | 37 |
| 7 | The Good Pagan's Failure | 45 |

### Part II

| | | |
|---|---|---|
| 8 | A New World Begins | 51 |
| 9 | Luther | 55 |
| 10 | Maimonides on Free Will | 61 |
| 11 | Thought | 71 |
| 12 | Lee Congdon on Russia | 75 |
| 13 | The Concept of Person | 81 |
| 14 | Purity in Aspiration | 87 |

### Part III

| | | |
|---|---|---|
| 15 | Rémi Brague | 95 |
| 16 | Yemima Ben-Menahem | 101 |
| 17 | On Human Worth and Excellence | 105 |
| 18 | Reconstruction | 109 |
| 19 | The Great Delusion | 117 |
| 20 | Physics and Philosophy | 123 |
| 21 | C. S. Peirce, Jacques Maritain, and Other Scholastics on the Problem of Induction | 139 |

## Part IV

| | | |
|---|---|---|
| 22 | Christopher Dawson and the Survival of Western Culture | 155 |
| 23 | George Santayana and Walter Lippmann | 159 |
| 24 | John T. Scott on Rousseau | 163 |
| 25 | Pierre Manent on Montaigne | 167 |
| 26 | Niki Kasumi Clements on John Cassian and Christian Ethical Formation | 171 |
| 27 | Alberto Boixados on Modern Art | 175 |
| 28 | Impossibility of a View from Nowhere | 179 |
| Bibliography | | 183 |
| Index | | 193 |

# Preface

This is a collection of essays and reviews written in the last decade that conveys a perspective on contemporary events and literature. They are written from a classical and Christian perspective, some may say, a Judeo-Christian perspective. They are collected because they convey a worldview much in need of restating at a time when Western society seems to have lost its bearings, not only in its legislative assemblies but in its judicial systems as well. Absent Christianity, we have become what we are. I write as a philosopher, specifically as one who has devoted most of his life to the study of metaphysics. For without metaphysics we do not have access to the immaterial dimension of life, or to the eternal. The hum-drum atomism once embraced by the ancients returned during the French Revolution with the Jacobians. In the following century, the empirical world of Hume, Locke, and Hobbes took hold, and with the aid of Kant it generated a truncated world view quite different from the one of previous centuries. It is the metaphysics of Plato, Aristotle, the Stoics, and Aquinas that opens one to God and provides one with a moral compass. But in the twentieth century, we find Karl Marx declaring religion to be the opium of the people, Sigmund Freud treating it as a psychotic illusion in need of cure, and John Dewey teaching that religion cannot be accepted uncritically even as a moral guide.

In a certain sense I write from a societal viewpoint. The relation between society and the individual is reciprocal. Families matter; so, too, does the noble individual. To that end, within the following pages I spend some time inquiring into the character of a few great men: George Washington, Charles De

Gaulle and Moses Maimonides. I draw upon and show respect for numerous contemporary authors who are engaged in research and analysis similar to mine. My intent is, with the aid of others, to restate some ancient but neglected truths. But more than that it is to show that true science is possible, that nature and human nature yield to human inquiry, that science is not to be confused with description and prediction. I write because I know that young people, often in contrast to their elders, are hungry for an alternative to the pedestrian materialism. I have found it so wherever I have lectured.

Jude P. Dougherty

# Acknowledgments

The composition and arrangement of the essays in this book were completed by the author before his passing from this life on March 6, 2021; some passages received minor alterations or the additions of citations in the course of editing for publication. The Dougherty family wishes to express its gratitude to The Catholic University of America Press—particularly Robert Harig and John Martino—for their assistance in these matters. We are confident that the author would be pleased with the results.

The family also hereby expresses thanks to those publishers who granted the author permission to re-use his work that had previously appeared in their publications. Chief among these is Peggy Moen, the editor of *The Wanderer* newspaper, in which pages appeared many of these chapters in an earlier form. Specifically, chapters 1–4, 6, 7, 11–13, 15, 17, 18, and 22–28 previously appeared in *The Wanderer* and are used with permission.

Portions of the introduction previously appeared in "Western Culture: A Collective Achievement," *Studia Gilsoniana* 8, no. 3 (2019): 751–78; the journal lists online a policy of granting copyright and publishing rights to its authors.

Chapter 5, "Washington's Solemn Contemplation," previously appeared as "How George Washington Anticipated and Warned of Our Present National Situation," *Catholic World Report*, February 21, 2022. It is reprinted with permission.

Chapter 8, "A New World Begins," previously appeared as "*A New World Begins: The History of the French Revolution* by Jeremy D. Popkin (review)," *Review of Metaphysics* 73, no. 3 (2020): 623–24. It is reprinted with permission.

Chapter 9, "Luther," previously appeared as *"Rebel in the Ranks: Martin Luther, the Reformation, and the Conflicts That Continue to Shape Our World*, by Brad S. Gregory (review)," *Annals of Cultural Studies* 11, no. 1 (2020): 81–84. It is reprinted with permission.

Chapter 14, "Purity in Aspiration," previously appeared as "Puritan Aspiration, Puritan Legacy: An Historical/Philosophical Inquiry," *Journal of Law and Religion* 5, no. 1 (1987): 109–23. doi:10.2307/1051020. The journal's policy is to allow authors to retain copyright and publishing rights.

Chapter 19, "The Great Delusion," previously appeared as *"The Great Delusion: Liberal Dreams and International Realities* by John J. Mearsheimer (review)," *Studia Gilsoniana* 8, no. 4 (2019): 893–99; as stated above, the journal holds a policy of granting copyright and publishing rights to the author.

Portions of chapter 20, "Physics and Philosophy," previously appeared in *The Nature of Scientific Explanation* (Washington, D.C.: The Catholic University of America Press, 2013), and are reprinted here with permission of the same Press.

Portions of chapter 21, "C. S. Peirce, Jacques Maritain and Other Scholastics on the Problem of Induction," have previously appeared in "An Aristotelian Account of Induction," *The Review of Metaphysics* 63, no. 4 (June 2010): 923–24, and *The Nature of Scientific Explanation* (2013). These excerpts are reprinted with permission.

A few chapters of this book have never been previously published. These are the preface, chapter 10 (Maimonides on Free Will), and chapter 16 (Yemimi Ben-Menahem). "Maimonides on Free Will" was however delivered in 2015 as an address to the Metaphysical Society of America.

# Introduction

"A Gothic Cathedral is a collective achievement, the outcome of countless craftsmen working across the centuries toward a common goal; it is not the arena for idiosyncratic personal expression."[1] So wrote Michael J. Lewis in an essay following the partial destruction of the Notre Dame Cathedral of Paris. Something similar may be said of an intellectual tradition that was being formed simultaneously with the coming into being of the European cathedrals.

Our subject is the formation of Western culture and the intellectual tools and social conditions that contributed to its formation. Stephen Gaukroger provides this insight: like those great cathedrals, modern science is the outcome of a distinctive culture, long in the making, a culture whose history begins in classical antiquity.[2] Presently and specifically, what needs to be rebuilt in concert with Notre Dame is a former Greek confidence in the human intellect's ability to reason to truths unseen, truths that acknowledge the immaterial character of human intellection, the spiritual component of human nature.

This book is an attempt through a series of interrelated essays to identify the essential features of Western civilization and its subsequent secularization in the aftermath of the French Revolution. These essays have been written in the context of an ongoing debate concerning the nature of the public philosophy that

---

1. Michael J. Lewis, "Rebuilding Notre Dame: Not So Fast," *Wall Street Journal*, May 1, 2019, https://www.wsj.com/articles/rebuilding-notre-dame-not-so-fast-11556744484.
2. See *The Emergence of a Scientific Culture: Science and the Shaping of Modernity, 1210–1685* (Oxford: Clarendon Press, 2006).

undergirds the freedom we take for granted. The approach is historical, something rarely attempted by contemporary philosophers who prefer to philosophize in an analytic mode or to limit themselves to textual exegesis or micro history, procedures that are often removed from the ongoing concerns of political and social life and have little to do with the pursuit of wisdom. A thesis that undergirds this investigation is that modernity cannot be understood apart from its break from classical antiquity.

A century ago, philosophers and literary intellectuals as diverse as Edmund Husserl, George Santayana, Alfred North Whitehead, and Paul Valéry, aware of the declining influence of Christianity, spoke of "the crisis of Western civilization." These and other scholars who followed them placed their hope in the revival of the classical sources of Western culture, with Valéry insisting, in addition, on an acknowledgment of a debt to Roman law and Roman Catholicism. Husserl and Santayana even in their prescience could not have imagined the diversity that confronts today's secularized Europe, a Europe that cannot control its borders or assimilate the flood of immigrants from the Middle East and Africa. At issue: absent a common core of conviction, can a nation maintain a rule of law?

When Oswald Spengler published his multivolume work, *The Decline of the West* (1926–28), few outside of professional circles understood his thesis or took the epitaph seriously. Today, almost a century later, no cultural historian can ignore the intellectual shift that took place in the second half of the twentieth century, one that has seriously eroded the spiritual resources that formerly animated Western culture.

The issue of cultural identity was similarly addressed from a historical perspective in a work published in 2001 by Samuel P. Huntington, who pointedly asks from an American perspective: "Who are we?" Starting from the premise that the United

States once possessed a common ethnic culture—one may say, an Anglo-Protestant soul—Huntington believes that somewhere between 1920 and 1970 it lost that soul, succumbing to a liberal virus that sapped its strength.[3]

Seventy-five years earlier, George Santayana had employed the same metaphor in speaking of the West when he wrote: "Our society has lost its soul. The landscape of Christendom is covered with lava, a great eruption of brute humanity threatens to overwhelm all the treasures that artful humanity has created."[4] Huntington is convinced that the United States remains an overwhelmingly Christian nation, yet he is not oblivious to the moral and cultural decline that he believes has weakened the moral fabric of the nation. He attributes that erosion not to gains made by non-Christian religions but to the increased prominence of a small but influential number of intellectuals and publicists, atheistic and materialistic, who in the name of multiculturalism have attacked the identification of the United States with its Christian founding and indeed with Western civilization itself.

In 1925, the distinguished American philosopher, Alfred North Whitehead, delivered the prestigious Lowell Lectures at Harvard University. Those lectures were subsequently published as *Science and the Modern World*.[5] The lectures were significant because for a predominantly American audience they challenged the Enlightenment view that only with the repudiation of the religious world view could modern science emerge

---

3. Samuel P. Huntington, *Who Are We? Challenges to America's National Identity* (New York: Simon and Schuster, 2001).

4. George Santayana, *The Winds of Doctrine* (New York: Charles Scribner's Sons, 1913), 5.

5. Alfred North Whitehead, *Science and the Modern World* (New York: Macmillan, 1925).

from the Dark Ages. Examining the relation between science and culture, Whitehead posed a fundamental question: Why did modern science emerge in the West in the sixteenth and seventeenth centuries when all the conditions required for its birth were seemingly in place in classical antiquity? Whitehead's attempt to answer his own question led him to examine the medieval and Renaissance background of modernity. Seven hundred years had elapsed between the fall of the Roman Empire and Newtonian physics. Whitehead's investigation led him to the conclusion that "the Middle Ages formed one long training in Western Europe in the sense of order. There may have been some deficiency with respect to practice, but the idea never for a moment lost its grip. It was predominately an era of orderly thought, rational through and through."[6] Whitehead goes on to attribute the medieval habit of definite and exact thought to the Greek philosophers, but in the passage quoted he is less interested in the metaphysics undergirding induction and inference than he is in the reciprocal influence of theory and practice. He writes: "Modern science derives from Rome (Monte Cassino) as well as Greece, and this Roman strain explains its gain in energy and of thought kept closely in contact with the world of facts."[7]

Lynn White Jr.—a professor of history at the University of California, Los Angeles—picks up this theme in an essay entitled "Dynamo and Virgin Reconsidered." This essay was a mere prelude to his massive study *Medieval Technology and Social Change*. "The chief glory of the Middle Ages," White declares, "was not ... its cathedrals, its epics, its vast structures of scholastic philosophy ... it was the building for the first time in his-

6. Whitehead, 13.
7. Whitehead, 19.

tory of a complex civilization which was upheld not on the sinews of sweating slaves and coolies but primarily by non-human power."[8] White goes on to say that the Rule of St. Benedict had much to do with a change in perspective regarding manual labor: "The monk was the first intellectual to get dirt under his fingernails."[9]

White's thesis is supported by the work of other scholars, notably Pierre-Maxime Schuhl and Benjamin Farrington. Schuhl wrote in the mid-decades of the twentieth century as chairman of the Sorbonne's philosophy department and as editor of the *Revue Philosophique*. Farrington is known for his multiple works on Greek science. Science—according to Farrington—whatever its ultimate development, has its origin in techniques, in the arts and crafts, in the various activities by which man keeps life going on. "Its source is experience, its aims practical, its only test that it works. Science arises in contact with things, it is dependent on the evidence of the senses. ... It requires logic and the elaboration of theory."[10] Finally, to understand science of any society is to be acquainted not only with its degree of material advancement but also with its political structure. "There is no such thing as science *in vacuo*," Farrington insists, "There is only the science of a particular society at a particular place and time."[11] Farrington goes on to say that the division of labor in Greek and Roman society actually retarded the development of the natural sciences. Both Whitehead and White agree. From the decline of Roman civilization

---

8. Lynn White Jr., "Dynamo and Virgin Reconsidered," *The American Scholar* 27, no. 2 (1958): 192.
9. White, 189.
10. Benjamin Farrington, *Greek Science: Its Meaning for Us*, vol. 1, *Thales to Aristotle* (Harmondsworth: Penguin, 1944), 14.
11. Farrington, 15.

until the rise of European universities in the twelfth century (a period of seven hundred years) the Benedictine monasteries came to play an important role in the development of Western culture and science, both as bearers of classical learning and as cultivators in their own right of science and technology.

The story may begin at Monte Casino, but one of Benedict's earliest disciples was Cassiodorus, one of the most learned men of his day, who lived from 490 to 585. In his advanced age, Cassiodorus founded the monastery of Vivarium on the family estate at Squillace. As a classicist, Cassiodorus saw the need for the preservation of ancient texts from Greece and Rome, texts which formed the minds of Justin Martyr, Athenagoras, and Clement of Alexandria—early Church Fathers—as they employed the writings of Plato, Aristotle, and the Stoics in their efforts to elucidate the teachings of the Gospels. With reason, Cassiodorus set his monks to copying those ancient texts. Though Benedict did not intend it, monasteries within his own lifetime had become—and were soon to be famous for—their scriptoria where the classics of antiquity were copied for posteriority. By the thirteenth century more than 700 monasteries had spread across Europe. Some were to be numbered among the great cultural centers of Europe. That story will be expanded in an essay that follows.

Responding to Samuel Huntington's observation about America's loss of its Christian soul, we find that Eric P. Kauffman—in covering the same ground as Huntington—agrees that America has lost its Protestant soul, but he believes that loss is a good thing, preferring the cosmopolitan, multicultural outlook that eradicates all religious and ethnic differences. Kauffman is convinced, contrary to Huntington's profile of contemporary America, that we as a nation have taken the secular multicultural outlook as our official creed. He finds overwhelming evidence of the multicultural spirit in school and university curricula, in the social sciences and in humanistic discourse, as well as in our political and legal systems. Today he could add its dominant presence in the media.

Given the social conditions described by the authors cited, the primary purpose of this volume is to determine how a shift in perspective so swiftly came about in the late nineteenth and early twentieth century, the shift from a Christian perspective to an agnostic or atheistic one. The players are as numerous as are the events which occurred. One of the earliest social theorists to address the consequences of that shift was Émile Durkheim, whose work will be considered at length. He wrote during a period when the social sciences were emerging under the influence of Auguste Comte, "the father of positivism," who is credited with giving the discipline of sociology its name. It was the period when the discoveries of Alfred Wallace, Charles Darwin, and Sigmund Freud entered the public conscience. The emergence of psychoanalysis and its effect on the common English vocabulary is described by Rudolf Allers in *The Successful Error*, a book that will subsequently be examined.

# Part I

## ☙ 1 ❧
# Becoming What We Are

HOW WE BECAME what we are. There are many explanations. One plausible account is found in the work of Rudolf Allers, who writes about the European intellectual landscape from 1850 to the opening decades of the twentieth century. Hegel and Nietzsche play their roles in shaping what we typically call "Modernity." From Allers we learn the meaning of the emerging disciplines—psychiatry, psychology, existentialism—as well as their varieties and exponents. We are exposed to the work of Gabriel Marcel, Ortega y Gasset, and others who tried to bridge or reconcile the gap between modernity and tradition.

Allers is best known for *The Successful Error*, a critical study of Sigmund Freud, and for *The Psychology of Character*. It is to be remembered that Allers in the company of Freud, Jung, and Adler are regarded as the founders of psychoanalysis, though Allers and Adler were soon to distance themselves from Freud. In rejecting Freud's materialism, Allers is nevertheless appreciative of the insight psychoanalysis has provided to those engaged in the treatment of mental illnesses. "Even the greatest errors of the human mind contain some truth,"[1] writes Allers. Our knowledge of the working of the human mind and our knowledge of human personality and character have been advanced because of psychoanalysis. Its contributions also include a psychology of sensation, elementary laws concerning

---

1. Rudolph Allers, *The Successful Error: A Critical Study of Freudian Psychoanalysis* (New York: Sheed and Ward, 1940), 217.

memory, the range of perception and apperception—notions all useful in education, sociology, and history. Freud's theory was initially advanced to enable the cure of neurotic patients, and later of mental illnesses generally. The existence of abnormal conduct raises the question of how to define normalcy, that is, human nature. We are told there were very few scientists or physicians prior to 1900 who were willing to consider strictly philosophical ideas such as human nature to be relevant.

During the nineteenth century the majority of psychiatrists regarded mental diseases as brain diseases. It was not science that suggested this idea, but philosophical materialism. Nor was it observation or empirical research that led to a greater emphasis on "striving," "appetition," "will," and "instinct" in the teachings of Griesinger and Meynert and later in Freud and Jung, but the agnosticism of Arthur Schopenhauer whose *The World as Will and Representation* proved to be highly influential at the time.

When psychology became a discipline in its own right in the second half of the nineteenth century, it offered little that was of use to psychiatry. What was needed was a theory of human nature that would encompass somatic as well as mental aspects and explain their relationship. Karl Jaspers abandoned psychiatry to become a philosopher. Rollo May and Ludwig Binswanger remained practicing psychiatrists while devoting considerable attention to philosophical questions. Jean-Paul Sartre in his *L'Être et le néant* devoted a long chapter to existential psychoanalysis. Mankind may have learned to master the external world of physical forces, improved his living conditions, and reached a much higher standard of living—but the question of what man is remained unanswered.

Freud prided himself on being scientific. Allers finds in Freud an optimistic faith in science to do what it cannot do. He did not recognize concepts or procedures except those used by the natural sciences. Given that science operates exclusively within the categories of material and efficient causality, Freud could not admit any "projective" or teleological principle—he could not admit of purpose in nature or human nature for such is not discernable. Biology remains a thorn, because it is difficult to deny that organs have their purpose within the whole. Darwin's theory of "natural selection" was then incorporated to account for the seemingly purposeful character of the organism.

It is generally conceded that psychoanalysis is effective in discovering the origin and the causes of mental states. But psychoanalysis may be questioned when it aims to explain the life of mankind, the evolution of culture, of religion, and of social phenomena. If in order to understand the true nature of mental phenomena, one may have to go back into the remote past of the individual—for nothing is ever totally forgotten—the concept may be misapplied if used to interpret social phenomena. Allers insists that psychoanalysis stands or falls on its materialist assumptions. If one is not a materialist, one cannot accept the Freudian outlook. Psychoanalysis is basically anti-Christian. This is seen when Freud speaks of Christianity as an "illusion," religion as "the neurosis of groups," and God as a "father figure." Seemingly, he was not aware of the enormous difference between the Jewish and Christian conceptions of God, nor of the pagan idea of a supreme god. In Allers's account, Freud "denies free will, ignores the spirituality of the soul . . . identifies mental with bodily phenomena, knows of no other end than bodily pleasure," and "is given to a confused but nevertheless obstinate subjectivism."[2] Such a philosophy does not have even one point in common with Christian thought.

2. Allers, *The Successful Error*, 199.

Allers is not alone in recognizing that a true account of human nature may await the recovery of classical antiquity. From Plato and Aristotle, modernity may learn that the immaterial or spiritual component of human nature is not empirically discerned but reasoned to from empirical evidence.

## ❧2❧
# Durkheim at the Founding of Social Science

"POPULISM" AS A TOPIC lends itself to interpretation. It is frequently used as a derogatory term, but it can be used to designate a political philosophy that supports the rights and powers of the ordinary citizen—as distinct from that of the elite who may govern them. To be specific, it may rightly designate the attitude of those who resist the deep state as found in Brussels and Washington, D.C. In any event, the topic offers an excuse to examine what may be called "Durkheim's Populism." Durkheim is not a household name, so let me explain why I have chosen him. Émile Durkheim was a French psychologist who lived from 1859 to 1917. If Auguste Comte can be called the founder of modern sociology, Durkheim may be called the father of modern psychology. His major works include *The Division of Labor* (1893), *Rules of Sociological Method* (1895), and a book entitled simply *Suicide* (1897). In common, their focus is social cohesion and the unity that only religion and education can provide.

Appointed to teach sociology and pedagogy at the University of Bordeaux in 1887, Durkheim published his doctoral dissertation (in English translation) "Montesquieu's Contribution to Social Science." That same year he created the journal *L'Année Sociologique*.

A question that has loomed large in intellectual circles for the last three quarters of a century is one that Durkheim asked himself, perhaps as early as 1904. Durkheim was aware that secularization in the aftermath of the French Revolution had changed the face of Europe. He asked how societies can maintain their coherence and integrity in an era when traditional and religious social ties no longer prevail. Put another way, absent Christianity, how is one to achieve a common moral outlook, a "common faith," as John Dewey was later to call it.[1]

Adam Smith's *The Wealth of Nations* was perhaps the first major work to address this issue. Lewis Coser, in his splendid introduction to the 1984 edition of Durkheim's *The Division of Labor*, provides this precis of Smith's view: "The emerging industrial form of production involved the gradual replacement of the artisanal mode of production, that is, a division of labor in which a particular producer, sometimes with the assistance of a few others, fashions a whole product, by a mode of production based on a much finer differentiation of tasks and activities than previously."[2] We know it today as the "assembly line." Does it matter? Historian J. G. A. Pocock provides this answer: "Society, organized as an engine for the production and multiplication of goods, is inherently hostile to society as the moral foundation of personality."[3] Marx saw that—at least in its capitalistic form—the new industrial division of labor alienated human beings from the product of their labor, as well as from their fellows. Given that "assembly line workers" are mere cogs in a wheel, the new mode of production, Marx maintained, is inherently inhumane.

---

1. John Dewey, *A Common Faith*, 2nd ed. (New Haven: Yale University Press, 2013).

2. Lewis Coser, introduction to *The Division of Labor in Society* by Émile Durkheim (New York: Free Press, 2014), xii.

3. J. G. A. Pocock, *The Machiavellian Moment: Florentine Political Thought and the Atlantic Republican Tradition* (Princeton: Princeton University Press, 1975), 301. Cited in Coster, introduction, xiii.

Durkheim may have wanted to enhance the autonomy of the individual in his social theory, but at the same time he found it necessary to examine the roots of social cohesion. The determination of the bonds that unite men with one another he assigned to the province of sociology.

Thus, Durkheim as a social scientist was led to explore how collective or group consciences are formed. Between 1898 and 1900, he published in the *Revue de Métaphysique et de Morale* three essays on the nature of morals and rights. These were expanded and developed and eventually published in 1937 and in English translation as "Professional Ethics and Civic Morals." Influenced by the positivist sociology of Saint Simon and Auguste Comte, and in accord with that methodology, Durkheim set about the empirical examination of social, moral, and psychological phenomena supporting a given community.

The science of morals, he insisted, must be based on the study of moral and judicial facts. These facts consist of rules of conduct that have been sanctioned by a given community. The sociologist may examine how these rules of conduct were established over the course of time, and determine the interests or causes that gave rise to them and the useful ends they fulfill. In his search for a communal set of beliefs that would replace what he thought was lost in the aftermath of the French Revolution, Durkheim was led to the study of religion in its most elemental form. That study did not lead him to the classical sources of Western culture for an understanding of religion, but to the study of primitive religions and totemism as he found it exemplified in Red Indian Pueblo rain dances and in the practices of aboriginal tribes in Australia.

One cannot fault Durkheim's method of investigation, but one must acknowledge its limitation. Durkheim may have had greater success had he chosen to study the mature forms of religion rather than the primitive. The God of Abraham, Isaac, and Jacob is not a totemic figure but a Creator responsible for the order of nature. Durkheim, lacking a metaphysics, is unable to reason to an immaterial order as did Plato and Aristotle or even to a Stoic conception of morality. Religion is left without a rational foundation.

Parenthetically, we may note that John Henry Newman—no stranger to British empiricism—in his early study of religion similarly devoted essays to the reasonableness of faith as it actually existed in the great mass of believers, subjecting it to what may be called a phenomenological analysis. Newman found in the common man a spontaneous movement of the mind, involuntarily culminating in an assent to God's existence. Such faith, he held, is an exercise of reason, the " acceptance of things as real, which the senses do not convey."[4] Charles Sanders Peirce, Newman's contemporary, argued much the same.[5]

Newman was convinced that the unbelief or skepticism promulgated by his agnostic contemporaries was not unlike the belief of Christians, insofar as unbelief or atheism, too, depends on presuppositions and prejudices—although of an opposite nature. Speaking of his contemporaries, Newman charged that typically the skeptic does not decide in accord with evidence, but instead considers the religious outlook so improbable that he does not have to examine the evidence for it. He cites David Hume's treatise on miracles as an example.

---

4. John Henry Newman, "The Nature of Faith in Relation to Reason," in *Fifteen Sermons Preached before the University of Oxford Between A.D. 1826 and 1843* (London: Longmans, Green, and Co., 1900), 207.

5. Editor's note: for a detailed comparison of Peirce and Newman, see Marial Corona, *The Philosophy of John Henry Newman and Pragmatism: A Comparison* (Washington, D.C.: The Catholic University of America Press, 2023).

In *La Division du Travail*, Durkheim acknowledges that social solidarity is a moral phenomenon that does not yield to precise observation and measurement. Yet he identifies two broad categories of traits: first, those that apply to all men and, secondly, those that apply domestically—that is, family obligations and civic duties such as loyalty and service to one's fellows. No man exists who is not a citizen of a state. Given the fact that human groupings are anterior to the birth of a human individual, the individual must be conceived as a component part of the social organism.

What rights does the human being possess at birth? Durkheim disputes the postulate that the rights of individuals are inherent. "It is not obvious that the rights of an individual are ipso facto his at birth. They are not inscripted in the nature of things."[6] "Rights have to be won in contest from opposing forces that deny them."[7] He is not alluding to conflicting claims on the public purse, but to something more fundamental. Among the forces that he finds suppressive of individual freedom are "those secondary groups of family, trade and professional organization, Church, regional areas, and so on."[8] As social life becomes more complex and varied, the state is obliged to intervene or provide a counter force to those entities because of their propensity to "absorb the personalities of their members."[9] The state has the obligation to check the domineering character of these secondary groups.

There must be no unchecked forming of secondary groups, for if they were left alone they would enclose the individual

---

6. Émile Durkheim, *Professional Ethics and Civic Morals*, trans. Cornelia Brookfield (London: Routledge, 1957), 65.
7. Durkheim, 65.
8. Durkheim, 65.
9. Durkheim, 65.

within their domain and separate him from the larger community. The state also has the obligation to rescue the individual from "patriarchal domination."[10] It is the state that organizes and makes rights a reality; "the stronger the State, the more the individual is respected."[11] The meaning of "self-government" is that choice is to be made according to the collective wisdom of the people, right or wrong. "A man is far more free in a throng than in a small coterie."[12]

Paul Mankowski, in reviewing Philip Eade's recent book on Evelyn Waugh for *First Things*, brings out an aspect of collective wisdom that is relevant to the theme of this essay. Waugh puts into the thought of one of his characters some insightful remarks. Rip is a protagonist in Waugh's short story "Out of Depth." In contemplating the future, Rip is aware that the future may not resemble the past. What if all the political and cultural solidities of twentieth century Europe were to disappear? What if everything taken for granted, every complacency, were demolished? Rip continues to muse: suppose "the contingencies of history have made conquering races out of the conquered," and suppose too, if the "new empires carry their civilizing schemes to the barbarian wilds that were once Piccadilly and Grosvenor Square"?[13] Under such circumstances, Rip sees that "only the spiritual realities remain unchanged."[14]

---

10. Durkheim, 64.
11. Durkheim, 57.
12. Durkheim, 61.
13. Paul V. Mankowski, "Waugh on the Merits," *First Things* (October 2017), review of *Evelyn Waugh: A Life Revisited* by Philip Eade (New York: Henry Holt, 2016).
14. Mankowski.

Rip is not depicted as a "pious, churchgoing" Londoner, "yet the unsensational gestures and rhythm of the Low Mass provide" for him "a touchstone of intelligibility, as Waugh puts it, 'a shape in chaos.'"[15] As a Catholic, Rip may feel at home anywhere in the world where the Mass is celebrated. Yes, in spite of the fact that, as Stuart Reid put it, "The suppression of the old liturgy [is] perhaps the greatest act of vandalism in history."[16] I cite this as an aspect of life that eludes Durkheim's positivistic method. Durkheim will maintain that "a successful society requires a general consensual agreement on the values that social efforts are designed to achieve."[17] Freedom cannot be secure in a society in which any substantial social element does not identify its own aspirations and self-interest with the good of the whole. Rousseau will speak of "a general will." Aristotle, by contrast, saw that if a true constitutional order, or a true polity, is to be brought into being, it must merge two opposing social tendencies: oligarchy, which may be defined as rule by the few for the few, and democracy, which is rule of the many for the benefit of the many. In the end Aristotle endorses a tripartite constitution.

George Mason, in drafting the Virginia Bill of Rights, follows this Aristotelian insight: representative government must represent the society it is called to govern. Mason saw that freedom cannot be secure in a society in which either a tyrannical majority or a tyrannical minority is able to impose its will on all who dissent from its dictums.

---

15. Mankowski.

16. Stuart Reid, "Church Cannon," *The American Conservative*, March 24, 2008, https://www.theamericanconservative.com/articles/church-cannon/

17. Charles M. Sherover, *From Kant and Royce to Heidegger: Essays in Modern Philosophy* (Washington, D.C.: The Catholic University of America Press, 2003), 213.

As Europe cedes the Continent to Islam, we may be aware but reluctant to accept the pessimism of prominent political theorists who try to envision what life might be like under an Islamic theocracy at odds with Christianity. We in the United States are beginning to face a similar fate as our institutions come under the influence of an intellectual cadre at war with Christianity. Absent a respect for the Constitution's Bill of Rights—absent a natural moral law—all decisions become political. Unless the U.S. Constitution holds, those who control the media are apt to determine the future of the country.

# ≈3≈
# Cicero

MARCUS TULLIUS CICERO, philosopher, orator, and statesman completed *De Senectute* (*On Old Age*), one of many books, in July 44 BC. Dedicated to Cato the Elder, the book addresses "the common burden of old age."[1] A beloved author through the ages, Cicero lived from 106 BC until he was murdered in 43 BC. Harvard University Press continues to make available William A. Falconer's 1923 laudable translation of *De Senectute* in its Loeb Classic Series. The book may be called "a timely treatise," given that the U.S. population grows significantly older with each passing generation. Authorities tell us that in 2018 seventeen per cent of the United States' GNP was devoted to health care, but there were only 7,000 certified geriatricians, about half the number said to be needed. Of course, care of the elderly is not exclusively limited to the physician. Nor is this treatise to be read only by health care givers or by the elderly. It is a time transcending moral or cultural treatise.

*De Senectute* is written in the form of a dialogue between Cato, Scipio, and Laelius, all presented as of old age, but it has an autobiographical character as Cicero draws upon his life's experience. Early in the essay, he remarks, "Philosophy, therefore, can never be praised as much as she deserves since she enables the man who is obedient to her precepts to pass every

---

1. Marcus Tullius Cicero, *De Senectute,* in *Cicero: De Senectute, De Amicitia, De Divinatione,* trans. William Armistead Falconer (London: William Heinemann, 1923), 11.

season of life free from worry."[2] Cicero acknowledges the disadvantage of old age, for old age withdraws us from active pursuits; it makes the body weaker; it deprives us of almost all physical pleasure; it is not far removed from death. Yet, "It is not by muscle, speed, or physical dexterity that great things are achieved, but by reflection, force of character and judgment; in these qualities old age is usually not only not poorer, but is even richer."[3]

Sapiens enters the dialogue saying, "I am wise because I follow Nature as the best of guides and obey her as a god; and since she has fitly planned the other acts of life's drama, it is not likely that she has neglected the final act as if she were a careless playwright."[4] Laelius adds, "Blame [any old age disadvantage] with character, not with age."[5] Some among the old lament because they are denied the sensual pleasure, without which they think life is not worth living. "[Those of] perversity and unkindly render irksome every period of life . . . the principles and practice of the virtues, which, if cultivated in every period of life, bring forth wonderful fruits at the close of a long and busy career . . . It is most delightful to have the consciousness of a life well spent, and the memory of deeds worthily performed."[6]

Cicero makes it clear that youth is not an unmitigated blessing; it can be a dangerous period of life. His reading of what he calls "foreign histories" teaches that the greatest states have been overthrown by the rashness of the young. Prudence is the harvest of age, Cicero will say in support, quoting Statius Cae-

2. Cicero, *De Senectute*, 11.
3. Cicero, *De Senectute*, 27.
4. Cicero, *De Senectute*, 13, 15.
5. Cicero, *De Senectute*, 17.
6. Cicero, *De Senectute*, 17, 19.

cilius, a Roman poet: "The saddest bane of age, I think, is this, that old men feel their years to be a bore to youth."[7] That may be so, but, "Life's racecourse is fixed; Nature has only a single path and that path is run but once, and to each stage of existence has been allotted its own appropriate quality."[8] Time and again, Cicero affirms that you enter old age as you have lived.

Granted that old age is devoid of strength, no strength is expected of it. There may be an exception insofar as Cicero recognizes an obligation. He takes these words from Caecilius: "If you ask a farmer, however old, for whom he is planting, he will unhesitatingly reply, 'For the immortal gods, who have willed not only that I should receive these blessing from my ancestor, but that I should hand them on to posterity.'"[9]

He advises the young to adopt a regime of health, to practice moderate exercise, to take just enough food and drink, to give their attention not solely to the body, for much greater care is due the mind and soul—for they too, like lamps, grow dim with time, unless we keep them supplied by oil. Exercise may cause the body to become heavy with fatigue, but intellectual activity gives buoyancy to the mind.

"Dotage" may be a characteristic of some but not of all. Cicero quotes from a speech given by Archytas of Tarentum, "'No more deadly curse,' said he, 'has been given by nature to man than carnal pleasure, through eagerness for which the passions are driven recklessly and uncontrollably to its gratification. From it comes treason and the overthrow of states; and from it spring secret and corrupt conferences with public foes. In short, there is no criminal purpose and no evil deed which

---

7. Cicero, *De Senectute*, 35.
8. Cicero, *De Senectute*, 43.
9. Cicero, *De Senectute*, 33.

the lust for pleasure will not drive men to undertake. Indeed, rape, adultery, and every like offence are set in motion by the enticements of pleasure and by nothing else.'"[10] Plato is said to have been in the audience when the lecture was given.

Steeped in the philosophy of Plato and Aristotle, Cicero stands at the foundation of what, through the centuries, has been called the natural law tradition. He affirms that there is an intelligible order in nature to which man is accountable. He speaks of the divine and eternal nature of the soul, a belief derived not solely by the force of reason and argument but also by the reputation and authority of philosophers of first rank. The soul has no source of motion, because it is self-moving. It is one substance; it cannot be divided and cannot perish.

The Church Fathers, especially Augustine, corrected from a Christian perspective doctrine that seemed to contradict Revelation. Cicero finds that this teleology is the product of a given order, includes the immortality of the human soul with hints of a bodily reunion, "corporeal returns to the visible constituents from which it came." In the closing pages of his treatise, Cicero writes: "O glorious day, when I shall set out to join the assembled host of souls divine and leave this world of strife and sin!"[11] And "indeed, I am eager to meet not only those whom I have known, but those also of whom I have heard and read and written."[12]

---

10. Cicero, *De Senectute*, 49.
11. Cicero, *De Senectute*, 97.
12. Cicero, *De Senectute*, 95.

# ❧4❧
# Larry Siedentop

IN THE OPENING PAGES of *Inventing the Individual: The Origins of Western Liberalism* historian Larry Siedentop, emeritus fellow of Keble College, Oxford, asks: Does it make sense to talk about the West? "People who live in the nations once described as part of Christendom—what many would call the post-Christian world—seem to have lost their moral bearings.... Some may welcome this condition, seeing it as liberation from historical myths such as the biblical story of human sin and redemption or a belief in progress 'guaranteed' by the development of science."[1]

Siedentop is convinced that, like it or not, we are in a period of competing beliefs, and it behooves us in the West to understand who we are.[2] The West is challenged on two major fronts, in Europe by Islamic fundamentalism—"a view of the world in which religious law excludes a secular sphere"—and elsewhere by Marxist socialism, transformed into quasi capitalism as in China.[3] He then asks whether "the West can still be defined in terms of shared beliefs," such as "liberalism."[4] Liberalism, he believes, has come to stand for "nonbelief—for indifference and permissiveness, if not for decadence."[5] If we are to understand

---

1. Larry Siedentop, *Inventing the Individual: The Origins of Western Liberalism* (Cambridge, Mass.: Belknap Press. 2014), 1.
2. Siedentop, 1.
3. Siedentop, 1.
4. Siedentop, 1.
5. Siedentop, 2.

ourselves, that is, understand the relationship between our beliefs and our social institutions, we must delve into history to determine what made us what we are, "to take a very long view."[6] Deep moral changes in belief, he acknowledges, can take centuries to develop and modify social institutions.

The book tells a fascinating story of how the "individual" became the organizing social principle in the West and how moral equality became protected before the law. "Today many people in the West today describe themselves as Christian, without regularly going to church or having even a rudimentary knowledge of Christian doctrine."[7] Siedenhop believes that this means that "people have a sense that the liberal secular world they live in . . . is a world shaped by Christian beliefs."[8] When Christianity is not acknowledged as foundational to the West, forgotten is the origin of the moral logic that joins Christianity with civil liberty. Human equality is not decreed by nature but by culture. The cultural and legal recognition of human equality is not simply told. Given the scope of this volume, a reviewer can only point to a few things that have elicited his interest and perhaps convey the tone of the volume.

In the first century after Christ we find St. Paul teaching that the "fatherhood of God" requires the "brotherhood of man," "seeing oneself in others and others in oneself."[9] Whereas men are not equally endowed by nature, they stand morally equal before God. By the second half of the third century, Christianity had become recognized as a component of the Roman Empire. Ambrose and Augustine had become major players. Augustine's

6. Siedentop, 2.
7. Siedentop, 3.
8. Siedentop, 3.
9. Siedentop, 65.

*City of God* became a template for an understanding of separate roles of civic and ecclesial authority. There were legacies from the past that had to be dealt with.

Siedentop insists that the ancient world was by no means secular. He identifies three inseparable customs inherited from pre-Roman antiquity: (1) domestic religion, (2) family, and (3) the right of property.[10] Every family had its hearth, its ancestors, and its gods, that is, gods "adored only by this family," gods who "protected it alone."[11] There was a crucial distinction between public and domestic spheres. The family was everything, a world in which obligation, gods, and priesthood were exclusively domestic.

At the core of such ancient thinking, Siedentop finds an "assumption of natural inequality."[12] The ancients "instinctively saw a hierarchy or pyramid. Different levels of social status reflected inherent differences in being. The paterfamilias, priest, or citizen did not have to justify his status. His superior status reflected his 'nature.'"[13] "Reason or logos provided the key to both social and natural order. Thought and being [and status], it was assumed, were correlative."[14]

Early chapters are devoted to the roles played by Charles Martel, Charlemagne, Gregory the Great, Benedict, and monasticism in the unification of Europe. Charlemagne was undoubtedly the most important. In a reign of nearly fifty years he "established Frankish control over most of Western Europe."[15]

10. Siedentop, 13.
11. Siedentop, 13.
12. Siedentop, 42.
13. Siedentop, 51.
14. Siedentop, 51.
15. Siedentop, 148.

Given the fall of the Roman Empire and the chaos that remained, Charlemagne attempted "to re-establish social order, create defensible frontiers, and suppress barbarism," a perennial threat.[16] Above all, he wanted to establish a Christian empire and "to propagate 'correct' beliefs and practices," which he regarded as the pre-condition for "order and unity."[17] To that end, with the help of Alcuin, he devoted resources to improving education for both the clergy and the people. In Siedentop's judgment, "Charlemagne presided over the last gasps of antiquity and the foundation of Europe."[18]

The Council of Reims (1049) decreed the protection of the poor, the sanctity of marriage, condemned consanguinity, and limited the power of the paterfamilias. Europe at the prodding of the Church was acquiring a moral identity. Pope Urban II's call to halt the spread of Islam revealed a Christian Europe. In Siedentop's estimation, "The crusades were a truly universal event, involving all strata of the population. They revealed 'a people' with a shared identity."[19] The murder of Thomas Becket of Canterbury "released powerful emotions across Europe."[20] "Within a few years, pilgrims from many countries began to make their way to the place of his 'martyrdom.'"[21]

Liberalism as a coherent doctrine, Siedentop maintains, was not born effortlessly. As a political system, it developed against the fiercest resistance of the Catholic Church. By the fifteenth century belief in moral equality, natural rights, rep-

---

16. Siedentop, 149.
17. Siedentop, 149, 150.
18. Siedentop, 150.
19. Siedentop, 194.
20. Siedentop, 195.
21. Siedentop, 195

resentative government, and the importance of free enquiry had come to be accepted. They were employed against the Church's claim to have a right to enforce Christian belief with the help of secular authorities. The Reformation put an end to confessional unity in Europe: religion came to be looked upon as "a matter for the private sphere, a matter of conscience."[22] Mounting opposition to the claims of the Church was fostered by the natural rights theory of Grotius and Hobbes and by the religious skepticism promoted, for example, by Montaigne's anticlericalism. Calls for toleration widened until it even included atheism. "The only birthright recognized by the liberal tradition is individual freedom."[23]

In the closing pages of the book, Siedentop asks whether Europeans will come to understand the moral logic that joins Christianity with civil liberty. It is a pertinent question. The freedoms Europeans take for granted are challenged as a result of the massive immigration of Muslims into Europe who desire to replace the laws of the states that received them with Sharia law. The old warfare between those of religious belief and "godless" secularism may have run its course. The religious camp eventually came to accept civil liberty and religious pluralism. The French anticlericals, with the exception of hard-line Marxists and writers such as Richard Dawkins, have given up on their attempt to extirpate religious belief. The new conflict between Christianity and Islam may be in principle irresolvable—a prospect that needs to be faced.

Siedentop has grounds to argue that in its origin, "secularism is Christianity's gift to the world."[24] From the time of St.

22. Siedentop, 334.
23. Siedentop, 349.
24. Siedentop, 360.

Paul, the belief in moral equality has implied a private sphere distinct from the civic—one in which each individual is "free to make his or her own decisions" apart from secular authorities.[25] That "sphere of conscience and free action," the joining of "rights with duties," finds its expression in the doctrine we know as separation of Church and state. "Secularism" in its ancient sense, Siedentop insists, "does not mean nonbelief or indifference," but rather "the conditions in which authentic beliefs should be formed and defended."[26]

---

25. Siedentop, 361,
26. Siedentop, 361.

## ❧5❧

# Washington's Solemn Contemplation

HE CALLED IT A "Solemn Contemplation," but it is better known as his "Farewell Address." It may be read profitably as a handbook for he who would govern. With admirable foresight, George Washington was aware of what the nation could experience if it failed to honor its charter documents. It was a magnificent speech. The first thing that the reader may notice is that Washington's learning, insight, and vocabulary are rarely encountered, if at all, in any public figure today.

George Washington saw as possible what many today would acknowledge as our present national situation. Washington feared the dissolution of the country, sectionalism—that is, Eastern, Southern, Western, the power of dissident minorities, and what we today call the "Deep State." Absent shared respect for the Constitution, he declared, we are no longer a people. It is the unity of government that constitutes us as one people. "The basis of our political systems is the right of the people to make and to alter their Constitutions of Government. But the Constitution which at any time exists, till changed by an explicit and authentic act of the whole people, is sacredly obligatory upon all."[1] It is

---

1. George Washington, "Washington's Farewell Address," September 19, 1796, available at https://www.mountvernon.org/education/primary-sources-2/article/washington-s-farewell-address-1796/. All quotations in this chapter come from this source unless otherwise noted.

"the duty of every citizen to obey the established government." Washington decries any activity that serves "to organize faction," any "extraordinary force" that aims to replace "the delegated will of the nation" with the "will of a party" or "a small but artful and enterprising minority of a community." He continues, "All obstructions to the execution of the Laws, all combinations and associations, under whatever plausible character, with the real design to direct, control, counteract, or awe the regular deliberation and action of the constituted authorities, are destructive of this fundamental principle, and of fatal tendency."

In common usage, the term "democracy" is far from a univocal term. "The People's Democratic Republic" is not what Woodrow Wilson had in mind when he led a crusade to make the world safe for democracy. For John Dewey, the leading American philosopher of Wilson's day, democracy is more than a form of government. It is a way of life, a creed directed to a social ideal.

While it is customary to distinguish among democracy's several forms—that is, direct, representative, social, and economic—what is usually meant by democracy is representative democracy. Direct democracy is identified with political life in ancient Greece, where policy decisions were made directly by the citizens as a whole, the majority determining the outcome. Apart from the New England town meetings initiated in the colonial period and continued today in some states, notably in Vermont and New Hampshire, the procedure is otherwise unknown, and the genuine town meetings that survive take place only where the body of citizens is small enough to enable participation by all. Referenda as employed in the United States in some way resemble the democracy of ancient Greece insofar as they seek the counsel of the populace as a whole, but they are often not binding and can be ignored by political authorities or reversed by courts.

Today when we call a form of government a democracy, we usually have in mind representative democracy in which citizens exercise their right to form policy, not in person but through representatives chosen by them. In a constitutional democracy, such as those that prevail in Europe and North America, the powers of the majority are exercised within the framework of a written constitution designed to protect the rights of the minority and the protection of other rights governing speech, press, and religion.

Viewed historically, a constitution need not be a single written instrument or even a legal document. Washington speaks of Thomas Jefferson's "founding essay." A constitution is likely to be more or less a formal acknowledgment of a commonly accepted set of fixed norms or principles recognized by all. St. Thomas, as well as Aristotle and Cicero before him, gave custom—rightly directed by the natural order—the force of law. Today the concept of a natural law is widely repudiated, and it would be foolish to declare that custom should reign unchallenged.

Greek democracy was a brief historical episode and is certainly not to be taken as the exemplar of modern democratic government. In contemporary political discourse, we hear much about the value of diversity, multiculturalism, and globalization. Yet diversity under a rule of law presupposes an accepted social order of society. In the United States the nineteenth century "melting pot" successfully blended elements of Christian Europe, but in the twentieth century and today, the melting pot is better described as a cauldron of unmeltable cultures.

The common Western liberal concept of democracy assumes uncritically that men are naturally and morally equal, an assumption that does not bear empirical scrutiny. Anyone who follows the course of events as reported daily by the media is aware that there is a wide disparity among the people, as a result of parental upbringing and education, that leaves the populace polarized in a way that is more fundamental than disparity of income. That is only one of many divisive factors. In many American states, the electorate is likely to contain undocumented aliens as well as legal immigrants. Both groups are likely to be deficient with respect to the English language, as well as ignorant of American history and Western political traditions.

The common faith that John Dewey sought as a foundation for American democracy has yet to be, nor is it likely to be. Absent a common core of beliefs, the self-government we take for granted is in jeopardy. Militating against democratic governance on both sides of the Atlantic is the indiscriminate awarding of suffrage to illegal immigrants, a politically biased media that limits access to vital information, an excessive tolerance of deviant behavior, the concomitant failure to punish the surrender of basic freedoms in the name of safety, and the docile acceptance of a bureaucratic imperium and a politicized judiciary. Undoubtedly the list could go on.

Washington presupposed virtue or morality in the people, "a necessary spring of popular government." He rhetorically asks, "Where is the security for property, for reputation, for life, if the sense of religious obligation desert the oaths, which are the instruments of investigation in Courts of Justice?" He answers, "Of all the dispositions and habits, which lead to political prosperity, Religion and Morality are indispensable supports." And adds, "Let us with caution indulge the supposition, that morality can be maintained without religion." What the future portends is beyond the scope of the present enquiry.

## ~6~
# Charles de Gaulle

JULIAN JACKSON ENDS PART ONE of his hefty volume, *De Gaulle*, with a quotation: "Without the Peloponnesian War, Demosthenes would have remained an obscure politician; without the English invasion, Joan of Arc would have died peacefully at Domrémy; without the Revolution, Carnot and Napoleon would have finished their existence in lowly rank; without the present war, General Pétain would have finished his career as the head of a brigade." The words are taken from a lecture by Charles de Gaulle. Then Jackson adds his own thought: "Without the Fall of France, de Gaulle would undoubtedly have become a leading general in the French army, probably a minister of defense, perhaps even head of the government—but he would not have become 'de Gaulle.'"[1] Jackson then takes 700 pages to prove it. Before examining the political and military issues confronting de Gaulle as the exiled leader of the Free French, we may look to the habits and character of the man himself.

Charles de Gaulle married Yvonne Vendroux, April 7, 1921. Both had inherited small sums from their deceased parents that enabled them to consider the purchase of a home. After searching for two years, they found a property at La Boisserie, Colombey-les-deux-Églises, in the Champaign region. Its price was 45,000 French francs, about the equivalent of a lieutenant's salary of 51,000 francs. Lacking an automobile of their own,

---

1. Julian Jackson, *De Gaulle* (London: Allen Lane, 2018), part 1, 99.

they depended on a friend to move them to their new home. The village itself had only one automobile. That belonged to the *garagiste*. The house was modest with minimal comforts; no running water for the first two years, no central heating, and electricity in only some of the rooms. The de Gaulles lived modestly throughout their married life even when occupying the stately structures that symbolized his authority.

De Gaulle was an avid reader. When assigned to a command post at Wangenbourg, Alsace, he ordered two books by Ernest Psichari and other books by Guy de Pourtalès on the lives of great composers, Wagner, Beethoven, Mozart, and Schubert. Even as president of France he read two or three books a week. He always read the winners of significant literary prizes. He admired Charles Péguy for his inclusive view of France and Emmanuel Mounier for his Christian personalism. He also wrote. His first book, in English translation, was entitled, *The Edge of the Sword* (1932). It sold 1,500 copies in the first year. Hitler read the book, annotating his copy. That was followed by *The Army of the Future* (1934) and *France and Her Army* (1938), a study of the way governments in different periods of history were able to forge an army "worthy of the role that France was destined to play."[2]

From the moment of his exile in 1940, de Gaulle regarded himself as the true incarnation of France, "faithful interpreter of the wishes and hopes of our people."[3] "I am a free Frenchman," he declared, "I believe in God and the future of my homeland. The Free French must avoid political partnership. Whatever anyone's beliefs and origins they must be a brother for all the others from the moment they begin serving France."[4]

    2. Jackson, *De Gaulle*, part 1, 79.
    3. Claude Bouchinet-Serreules, quoted in Jackson, *De Gaulle*, part 2, 17.
    4. Charles De Gaulle, quoted in Jackson, *De Gaulle*, part 2, 17.

De Gaulle was forty-nine when he arrived in London on June 17, 1940. After some mishap, his family arrived from Bordeaux on June 20 and found accommodation at Hotel Rubens near Buckingham Palace. His son, Philip, later remembered that it was the only time he had ever seen his parents kiss in public.

The correspondence between de Gaulle and Maritain is sparse, but worth noting. Both agreed that France was not only engaged in a military conflict but in a spiritual struggle as well. In January 1941 de Gaulle wrote to Maritain, "Like you, I believe that our people are suffering from a kind of moral collapse. I thought that to climb out of the abyss the first thing was to prevent people from resigning themselves to infamy and slavery. . . . I think that we will have to profit from the national reassemblement around pride in ourselves and resistance to lead the nation toward a new democratic ideal."[5]

In November 1941, Maritain wrote to de Gaulle to the effect, given the fact that the bourgeoisie had betrayed France, that the country needed a "new regime 'reconciling Christianity and liberty, i.e., the tradition of St. Louis and the tradition of the Declaration of the Rights of Man.'" De Gaulle wrote back, "I am not worried for the future of democracy. Its enemies are only ciphers. I do not fear for the future of religion. The bishops have behaved badly but there are good cures, simple priests, who are saving us. . . . All that is healthiest in France is to be found in the people."[6] De Gaulle was not enthusiastic about the reforms of Vatican II. He worried that Pope John XXIII had been unduly influenced by a Vatican group who wanted to revolutionize everything. "I am not sure the Church was right to suppress

---

5. De Gaulle, quoted in Jackson, *De Gaulle*, part 2, 49.
6. Jacques Maritain and De Gaulle, quoted in Jackson, *De Gaulle*, part 2, 17.

processions . . . and the Latin service. It is always wrong to give the impression of denying oneself and being ashamed of what one is. How can you expect others to believe in you if you do not believe in yourself?"[7] When President Mitterrand in 1965 proposed that the contraceptive pill be legalized, de Gaulle objected, "One must not reduce women to machines for making love! This goes against all that is most precious in women: fecundity. A woman is made to have children! If one tolerates the pill nothing will hold sway anymore! Sex will invade everything."[8]

From Jackson's copious account, we learn much about Europe's political struggles during the interim war years and much more about the years between September 1939 and June 1945. When de Gaulle arrived in London, Jacques Maritain, at that time living in New York, was the most famous Frenchman in exile. Maritain advised de Gaulle to confine himself to a symbolic role rather than try to form a government in exile. De Gaulle begged to differ. "Men cannot do without being led any more than they can do without eating, drinking and sleeping. Leaders have to be able to stir the imagination and excite the latent faith of the many."[9] This he did in his nightly broadcasts from London.

De Gaulle regarded the Vichy government of General Petain as collaborationist and he declared that he was the true leader of the Free French. The Vichy government responded in 1940. To rally the Free French in what remained of the Western Empire, de Gaulle spent six weeks in Africa. Jackson describes it as an "epiphany," for de Gaulle was lauded and cheered wherever he went. In Brazzaville and Gabon he discovered he

---

7. De Gaulle, quoted in Jackson, *De Gaulle*, part 2, 78.
8. De Gaulle, quoted in Jackson, *De Gaulle*, part 2, 78.
9. De Gaulle, quoted in Jackson, *De Gaulle*, part 1, 73.

was a living legend. As he recalled the experience: "There was a person named de Gaulle who existed in other peoples' minds, a separate personality from myself."[10] He was emboldened by that public perception. While in Brazzaville, he issued a manifesto, setting up an Empire Defense Council and exercising powers in its name, in the name of France.

With the German defeat at Stalingrad in 1943, it was clear that the war had turned decisively in favor of the Allies, and at some point a landing in France would be attempted. To prevent France from falling into the hands of the communists, de Gaulle formed a provisional government which he would lead from 1944–46. He had come to the conclusion early in 1940 that the only way to save France was to leave France. With the aid of his lectures on BBC and the support of Churchill, de Gaulle imposed himself as the only public voice to offer an alternative view to that of Pétain. On June 28, 1940, Churchill agreed officially to recognize de Gaulle as the leader of the Free French. De Gaulle may not have been a natural orator, but the oddity of his delivery and diction gave an extra weight to his speeches.

With Liberation in 1945, de Gaulle became provisional president of the Fourth Republic. When the nation was forced to choose the kind of political system it would adopt, de Gaulle advocated a presidential rather than a parliamentary one. The issue was put to a referendum. In resigning his provisional role, he expected that public support would bring him back to power with a mandate for his preferred mode of governance, but the National Assembly chose instead, Felix Gorin. The history of the Fourth Republic is one of inter-party feuding, inaction, and chaos.

In 1958 de Gaulle came out of retirement at the request of the National Assembly to deal with the crisis brought on by the

10. De Gaulle, quoted in Jackson, *De Gaulle*, part 2, 17.

Algerian War. He was appointed prime minister by René Cote and charged by Cote to rewrite the Constitution of France, which became the foundation of the Fifth Republic. He was elected president later that year and reelected in 1965, a position he held until his retirement to Colombey in 1969.

When de Gaulle was elected President of the Fifth Republic in 1958, Jean-Paul Sartre was violent in his anti-Gaullism. *Le Monde* had become the voice of the progressive left. The only significant "intellectual" to support de Gaulle was Francois Mauriac. As an early biographer of de Gaulle, Mauriac wrote: "As a Christian I feel confirmed in my certainty that de Gaulle is not a man of destiny; he is a man of divine grace."[11] Mauriac's biography, it may be noted, was so effusive in its assessment of de Gaulle's achievements that even Mauriac's admirers thought of it as a hagiography.

On November 2, 1964, All Saints Day, Charles and Yvonne went as they did annually to pay their respects at the grave site of their daughter Anne. On November 9 de Gaulle worked as usual, interrupting his day's work by two brief walks. He took tea with his wife and was writing some family letters when he shouted in pain and slumped on the table. Yvonne called the doctor and the village priest. De Gaulle received the last rites before he died at 7:25 p.m. Yvonne had the body laid out in the center of the room, dressed him in his uniform, and covered the body with the tricolor. On the table at his bedside were two candles, a crucifix, and a cup of holy water, usually provided for the priest administering the last rites. She placed in his hands

---

11. Francois Mauriac, *Bloc-notes*, vol. II: 1958–1960 (Paris: Seuil, 1993), 378 (01/30/1960), cited in Jackson, *De Gaulle*, 648.

a rosary that had been given to him by Pope John XXIII. Yvonne maintained a silent vigil through the night and released the news of his death the next morning.

In 1940, Jacques Maritain may have been critical of de Gaulle's attempt to form a government in exile, but by 1942 his reservation had given way to the recognition that de Gaulle's refusal to accept defeat was "a sort of heroic chivalry" that gave "back hope to the French."[12] Julian Jackson recalls Maritain's words with approval: "Now that the rancid arguments of the Vichy apologists are long past, there cannot be a French citizen who does not recognize the truth of Maritain's statement and who does not feel justifiably proud of their country as a result of what de Gaulle achieved between 1940 and 1944. He saved the honor of France."[13] Jackson's magnificent account of this great man is equal to the man himself.

12. Jacques Maritain in Antoine de Saint-Exupéry, *Ecrits de guerre, 1939–1944* (Paris: Gallimard, 1982), 275–81, cited in Jackson, *De Gaulle*, 777.

13. Jackson, *De Gaulle*, 777.

## ❧7❦
# The Good Pagan's Failure

THE GOOD PAGAN'S FAILURE is the title of a book first published in 1939 by Rosalind Murray. It is an indictment of Western liberalism. Readers of a certain age will remember that Rosalind was the daughter of Gilbert Murray, the distinguished Oxford professor of Greek and Classical Studies, who in my youth was the object of compulsory study. For a time, Rosalind Murray was the wife of Arnold Toynbee, the celebrated author of the twelve volume *A Study of History* (1934–1965). Given the British literary circles in which she moved, Murray knew well the pagan mind of which she wrote.

The pagan of her day was likely to be a philosophical materialist, an empiricist who denied a natural order to which he might be accountable. Murray's liberal was a mild sort, living comfortably within an inherited culture and a moral order he did not create and whose principles he could not defend. Unlike the pagan of antiquity, he denies the existence of a divinely scripted natural order. The pagan of antiquity did not, as the modern liberal has done, reject Christ. The pagan did not know Christ, but the modern liberal has known Christ and has rejected Him. Murray is blunt: "The contemporary world is atomic in its outlook," governed by "disassociated ideas, emotions, sense impressions."[1] We do not look to the modern liberal for moderation and wisdom, or for kindness and good sense.

---

1. Rosalind Murray, *The Good Pagan's Failure* (New York: Longmans, Green, and Co., 1948), 7.

Rosalind Murray's book came to mind as I read Lionel Barber's interview of Vladimir Putin in the June 26, 2019, edition of *The Financial Times*. Given its province, the interview was mainly about the hopes Putin held for the G-20, which was about to occur, and Putin's reflections on the twenty years that he has been in the upper echelons of the Russian Federation's governing body. In response to Barber's question, "Do you believe that the world now has become more fragmented?" Putin replied, "During the Cold War . . . there were at least some rules that all participants in international communication more or less adhered to or tried to follow. Now, it seems there are no rules at all. In this sense, the world has become more fragmented and less predictable, which is the most important and regrettable thing."[2] The interview goes on to discuss Russia's relationship with Japan, China, OPEC, the United States and North Korea. Speaking of the last, Putin opined, "What we should be talking about is not how to make North Korea disarm, but to how to ensure the unconditional security of North Korea and how to make any country, including North Korea feel safe and protected by international law that is strictly honoured by all members of the international community." Of President Trump, whom he clearly respects, Putin said, "I think that he is a talented person. He knows very well what his voters expect from him."

Putin's view of U.S. foreign policy is far from positive. "It is impossible to impose current and viable French or Swiss democratic standards on North African residents"; "the region has known only monarchies with a system similar to that which

2. Vladimir Putin, interview by Lionel Barber, *The Financial Times*, June 26, 2019, https://www.ft.com/content/878d2344-98f0-11e9-9573-ee5cbb98ed36

existed in countries such as Libya." He goes on to say, "They tried to impose something that they had never known or even heard of. All this led to conflict and intertribal discord. In fact, a war continues in Libya." Several times during the interview, Putin sought to address a number of cultural issues, but Barber put him off until the near end of the interview. Putin was finally allowed to make the point that, "The liberal idea has become obsolete. It has come into conflict with the interests of the overwhelming majority of the population." Looking at both Europe and America, Putin said, "The liberal idea presupposes that nothing needs to be done. Migrants can kill, plunder and rape with impunity because their rights as migrants must be respected. What rights are these? Every crime must have its punishment."

When asked, "You have seen many world leaders. Who do you most admire?" Putin responded, "If you mean any present-day leaders from different countries and states, of the persons I could communicate with, I was most seriously impressed by former president of France, Chirac. He is a true intellectual, a real professor, a very level-headed man as well as very interesting. When he was president, he had his own opinion on every issue, he knew how to defend it and he always respected his partner's opinions." In those words of tribute to President Chirac, perhaps Vladimir Putin was describing how he sees himself.

The interview finally got around to a discussion of the liberal assault on religion and the role of religion in society. "[Religion] should play its current role," Putin insists, "It cannot be pushed out. . . . Russia is an Orthodox Christian nation, and there have always been problems between Orthodox Christianity and the Catholic world." Putin noted that today there may be problems in the Catholic Church, but they should not be over exaggerated or used to destroy the Roman Catholic Church itself. "This is what cannot be done," he said. "Sometimes, I get the feeling that these liberal circles are beginning to use certain elements and problems of the Catholic Church as a tool for destroying the Church itself. This is what I consider to be incorrect and dangerous."

Putin added, "Have we forgotten that all of us live in a world based on biblical values? Even atheists and everyone else live in this world. We do not have to think about this every day, attend church and pray, thereby showing that we are devout Christians or Muslims or Jews. However, deep inside, there must be some fundamental human rules and moral values. In this sense, traditional values are more stable and more important for millions of people than this liberal idea, which, in my opinion, is really ceasing to exist." Barber responds, "So . . . religion is not the opium of the masses?" Putin replies, "No, it is not." Religious authorities have made that point time and again, but who among Western political leaders has come anywhere close to affirming Putin's assessment?

# Part II

## 8

# *A New World Begins*

"THE HISTORY OF THE SECULARIZATION of modern culture has yet to be written," so wrote Christopher Dawson in 1972.[1] It is doubtful that he could say that today. The latest attempt to write that history is that of Jeremy D. Popkin, whose *A New World Begins: The History of the French Revolution* was published in late 2019. Dawson himself, in several essays, addressed the intellectual revolution that he believed had taken place in France decades before the political one. He followed a minority movement composed of philosophers and literary intellectuals that gradually claimed wider circles until its adherents won key positions of social and intellectual influence. Popkin confirms Dawson's supposition with historical detail and vivid portraits of the principals.

Over a long career Popkin has authored more than a dozen books as well as numerous articles. He has been honored by prestigious lectureships in North America and Europe. His recent works include *From Herodotus to H-Net: The Story of Historiography* and *Revolutionary News: The Press in France, 1789–1799*.

As Popkin's narrative develops, names run by: Diderot, d'Alembert, Voltaire, Montesquieu, Rousseau, Danton, Robespierre, Carnot, Duchène, Montagne, and Saint-Just. Most were contributors to the *Encyclopedie* (1751–1772). They comprised a generation of thinkers who rejected much of the political and

---

1. Christopher Dawson, *The Gods of the Revolution* (Washington, D.C.: The Catholic University of America Press, 2015), 13.

religious assumptions of their day. In Popkin's words: "The subversive originality of the *Encyclopedie* was to present the ideas of the great minds of eighteenth-century French letters as if they were simply common sense."[2] Additionally, Voltaire campaigned against revealed religion, Montesquieu's *Spirit of the Laws* challenged the established political order, and Joseph Fouché—a leader of the Jacobians—typified those who wished to de-Christianize France.

Popkin offers a sympathetic portrait of Louis XVI and his efforts to maintain a tradition that he believed was his sacred duty to preserve against the claim that "everything must change." With the royal treasury in bankruptcy, the monarchy was on the verge of collapse. On the advice of Charles Alexandre de Calonne, the king consented to call in 1786 an Assembly of Notables. Calonne offered tax paying landowners a vote in decision making. They would be allowed to participate in the decision-making process and on their own elect provincial assemblies. The Notables at that time included seven princes of the blood who stood in the line of royal succession, fourteen prelates, an impressive contingent of dukes and peers representing the military, and marquises, including the young Lafayette. When Calonne proposed new taxes, the Notables were wary. His sweeping proposals threatened the special interests of the privileged groups from which the Notables were drawn. It would require the Estates General to approve new taxes. Given the stubborn opposition to Calonne's proposed reforms, the king dismissed the Assembly.

The organization of a Third Estate soon followed. The Third Estate represented commoners and the lower clergy and met in

---

2. Jeremy D. Popkin, *A New World Begins: The History of the French Revolution* (New York: Basic Books, 2019), 50.

defiance of the king's orders to disperse. On the tennis courts of Versailles, deputies attending took an oath not to disband until a new French Constitution had been adopted. The Third Estate declared itself to be the National Assembly. Louis recognized the legitimacy of the National Assembly but then surrounded Versailles with troops and dismissed Jacques Necker, a popular minister of state who was a leader of the reform movement. In response Parisians stormed the Bastille, thus setting the revolution in motion. Popkin writes, "Virtually all historians agree that [the Revolution] resulted from frustrations of a rising 'bourgeois class determined to challenge a feudal order that stood in the way of political and economic progress."[3] He goes on to identify three stages of the revolution: 1) the session of June 17, when the deputies named themselves the "National Assembly" and asserted the right to make the nation's laws, 2) the revolution of July 14 when the population of Paris stormed the Bastille and symbolically destroyed the authority of the king, and 3) August 4, when the National Assembly abolished the feudal system.

On December 25, 1793, Robespierre delivered a speech to the Committee on Public Safety laying out the principles of revolutionary government. What Popkin calls "The Arc of Terror" followed from January 1973 to July 1794. The king was judged guilty of foreign entanglements and executed on January 21. Marie Antoinette was executed nine months later.

In 1794, the Convention delegated authority to the Committee on Public Safety. The Paris tribunal sent 1,300 to their deaths, including public figures such as Guillaume-Chrétien de Lamoignon de Malesherbes, a reformist former minister who was targeted for having volunteered to defend Louis XVI's

3. Popkin, *A New World Begins*, 2.

life at his trial, the chemist Antoine Lavoisier, poet *André Chénier*, and the Archbishop of Paris, Jean-Baptiste Gobel. No citizen could be sure he would be alive the next day. The Terror had turned into an irrational and uncontrollable bloodbath. Any trace of opposition to the regime was considered evidence of conspiracy.

Popkin writes: "Even in hindsight it is difficult to say the basic achievements of the Revolution could have been preserved in 1793 without something representing revolutionary dictatorship."[4] The stage was set for Napoleon, a story that Popkin tells with authority, but one that will not be pursued here. Given its historical detail and vivid portraits, it is difficult to see how Jeremy Popkin's *A New World Begins: A History of the French Revolution* is likely to be surpassed.

---

4. Popkin, 417.

## ~9~
# Luther

THAT THE REFORMATION ENDED the Middle Ages and prepared the way to modernity is a thesis defended by Brad S. Gregory, Professor of History at University of Notre Dame. Gregory maintains that the Reformation had the long-term effect of gradually and unintentionally transforming Europe from a world permeated by Christianity to one in which religion would be separated from public life. Drawing upon the sources utilized in his previously published *The Unintended Reformation*, Brad Gregory provides an in-depth portrait of Martin Luther and his life and intent in *Rebel in the Ranks: Martin Luther, the Reformation, and the Conflicts That Continue to Shape Our World*.

In September 1517 Luther published a one-page broad sheet entitled "A Disputation against Scholastic Theology." He condemned theologians who make use of "Wretched Aristotle": "No one can become a theologian unless he becomes one without Aristotle. . . . [T]he whole Aristotle is to theology as darkness is to light."[1] Luther was not alone in objecting to scholastic theology. Erasmus of Rotterdam, usually identified as a Renaissance humanist, mocks scholastic theologians for their arcane jargon in his *Praise of Folly* (1511).[2]

---

1. Martin Luther, "Disputation against Scholastic Theology," in *Luther's Works*, ed. Helmut T. Lehmann, vol. 31, *Career of the Reformer: I*, ed Harold J. Grimm (Philadelphia: Muhlenberg Press, 1957), 12. Cited in Brad S. Gregory, *Rebel in the Ranks: Martin Luther the Reformation and the Conflicts That Continue to Shape Our World* (New York: HarperOne, 2017), 39.

2. Erasmus like Luther acknowledged deviant practices in the Church. A faithful Catholic priest, he is known as a Renaissance humanist and a translator of the New Testament.

The publication of his Ninety-Five Theses turned Luther into a public figure. His *Disputation against Scholastic Theology* a few weeks before had not brought him much notice, for it concerned matters in which only theologians would likely have been interested. The Ninety-Five Theses, however, addressed popular practices related to the Church's teaching.

At the time he published his famous theses, Luther assumed rather than rejected papal authority. He recognized that indulgences are legitimate, that purgatory is real, and that intercessory prayer is efficacious. Luther's main target at the time was the careless dispensation of indulgences by reckless preachers. It is when he addressed issues related to human sinfulness, namely God's forgiveness and the ideal Christian life, that a distinctive theology began to emerge. Human beings, Luther argued, needed to be made aware of their complete inability to assist in their own salvation. This claim contradicted traditional Catholic teaching and could not be ignored by the papacy.

The first papal reaction was to handle Luther quietly within his own religious order. At the prompting of Pope Leo X, the head of the Augustinian order made inquiries to determine if Luther was preaching "novelties." Under questioning, Luther sought to know why his teaching was considered wrong. Brad Gregory tells us, "Except for his continuing disdain for scholastic theology, Luther's teaching remained traditional in its reliance on canon law, the church fathers, and scripture."[3]

Pope Leo nevertheless gave Luther sixty days to appear in Rome for questioning. The Elector, Fredrick III of Saxony, prevented Luther from going. Gregory noted that this was the first instance of political protection accorded Luther, and he sug-

---

3. *Rebel in the Ranks*, 53.

gested that without that protection Luther's subsequent rise to fame would not have occurred.

Given that Fredrick prevented Luther from going to Rome, Pope Leo then sent Thomas de Vio (better known as Cajetan), a distinguished interpreter of Thomas Aquinas, to investigate. Cajetan did not find Luther to be a heretic, but he did find his ideas about faith to be "weird," Gregory writes.[4] Luther insisted that no one can be justified except by faith. Without faith all other things are acts of presumption and desperation. In debate Luther held firm, "I do not want to be compelled to affirm something contrary to my conscience, for I believe without the slightest doubt that this is the meaning of Scripture."[5] Scripture's authority, Luther insisted, supersedes papal authority. The pope is not above but under the Word of God. The repository of God's revelation is Scripture alone. All other authorities—popes, councils, church fathers, theologians—are subordinate to it.

It was agreed that Luther's theses would be publicly debated before relevant theological faculties of Erfurt and Paris. At a meeting in June 1519, two hundred scholars were in attendance, including some rowdy students. In the course of 1518, Luther had written forty-five different treatises and over eighty editions of his works appeared in the same year. In the following year that number doubled. In his work entitled "The Papacy at Rome: A Treatise on Good Works," Luther charges that popes, bishops, and priests are princes of the devil's army. Satan himself has conquered the papacy and installed the Anti-Christ on

---

4. *Rebel in the Ranks*, 56.

5. Martin Luther, *Proceedings at Augsburg*, in *The Annotated Luther*, vol. I, *The Roots of Reform*, ed. Timothy J. Wengert (Minneapolis: Fortress Press, 2015), 147, cited in *Rebel in the Ranks*, 57.

the Papal Throne. Rome responded with the papal bull, *Exsurge Domine*, condemning forty-nine propositions attributed to Luther, including "the priesthood of all believers."

In a treatise, "To the Christian Nobility," Luther exhorted German political leaders to take up twenty-seven measures to reform the Church. Many of these imperatives concerned ending the procedures by which money is extracted by Rome. Other of his directives advocated rejection of the practices and teaching characteristic of medieval Christianity, such as pilgrimages understood as works of devotion. "The endowing of friaries should likewise end; the clergy should be allowed to marry. . ." the list goes on: "saints' days should be turned into working days; all the Church's fasting regulations and dietary restrictions should be left to individual discretion; pilgrimage chapels should be destroyed; the canonization of saints should cease; confraternities should be prohibited; the university teaching of Aristotle's ideas about human beings, nature, and ethics should stop; canon law should be abolished. It was clear that the implementation of these changes would alter Christian life beyond recognition—which was exactly Luther's point."[6] Johann Eck had trouble getting the papal bull posted. Disruptions accompanied the publicly posted *Exsurge Domine*. Yet, Luther did not reject the established Church in principle; he rejected it because papal authority contradicted his understanding of God's Word. Christians needed liberation from a despotic Church. The papal court was more corrupt than Babylon or Sodom.

According to Luther, no one can live up to God's standards. Salvation is something God gives you freely at birth. The rest depends on faith. Liberated by faith from the impossibility of meeting God's standards for salvation, you no longer need to

6. *Rebel in the Ranks*, 56.

be worried about it. God has already bestowed it upon you. You are thus free to focus upon your neighbor and his needs. You are bound to do so as an expression of your faith.

By 1520, Luther, in the "Freedom of Christianity"—no longer pursuing reform within an existing Church—called for a revolution in the name of God's Word. Luther was finally declared a heretic in 1521.

In Brad Gregory's judgment, the Reformation is a paradox, a religious revolution that led to the secularization of society. The individualism and the liberalism that flowed from Luther's teaching led to a conception of society in which you can believe whatever you want, live however you wish within the laws of the state, and so can everyone else. The first unintended consequence of the Reformation was the proliferation of many rival versions of Protestantism. Disagreement about Christian doctrine mattered because religion informed politics, law, economics, education, social relationships, family life, morality, and the culture at large. Most civic leaders believed that unity of belief was a condition of successful government.

From the perspective of the state, religion had to be redefined and its scope narrowed. Under the influence of Descartes, Locke, and Hobbes, Holland in 1581 outlawed Catholic worship altogether. In Amsterdam, believing Catholics could practice their faith behind closed doors, subject to the payment of a fee.

In 1614 the Dutch began colonizing what became the British colonies between New England and the Chesapeake Bay. Nine of the new colonies established churches, but only in Virginia did the Church of England become the established Church. Absent religious restraints, many Puritans, abandoning the position of their predecessors, participated in the Atlantic slave trade.

## ❧10❦

# Maimonides on Free Will

I SPEAK TODAY about a medieval author whose neglected work is not without interest even today.[1] He is the Jewish philosopher and theologian Moshe ben Maimon (1135–1204), known in the West as Maimonides. His two great works are the *Mishneh Torah* (fourteen volumes), a codification of Jewish law considered to be Maimonides's magnum opus, and the better-known philosophical work, *Guide for the Perplexed*. It is the latter that I will draw upon principally, although I will say something about the *Mishneh Torah*. His medical treatises constitute an important chapter in the history of medicine but are beyond the scope of this presentation.

The *Mishneh Torah* consolidated and codified an array of Jewish halakhah rules and norms and set them in a unified and accessible structure without the usual back-and-forth discussion of opinions, major and minor, that characterizes the *halakhah* of the period. Maimonides sought to reinterpret Judaism, in the words of one commentator, "as a religion suited to the sensibilities of philosophical religiosity and to create a unified and accessible *halakhah* that would be accepted by all Jewish communities, wherever they may be."[2] No mean feat, Moshe Halbertal reminds the reader, given that "by its very nature, the Jewish tradition contains a streak of

---

1. An address given at the University of Georgia, April 2015.
2. Moshe Halbertal, *Maimonides: Life and Thought,* trans. Moshe Halbertal (Princeton: Princeton University Press, 2014), 363.

stubborn resistance to the setting of shared, binding, principles of belief."[3]

Maimonides, a native of Cordoba, Spain, belonged to the school of Aristotle and his Muslin interpreters, notably al-Farabi, Avicenna, and Averroes. In all of his writings, philosophical as well as halakhic, Maimonides took science and philosophy, which he often refers to simply as "wisdom," as the medium for attaining the heights of religious experience, namely, the love and awe of God.

Before I examine some key elements of his teaching, I must say something about these great philosophers and the world they inhabited. Medieval Europe did not inherit Greek philosophy directly from Greece but indirectly through the channel of Syrian, Persian, and Arabic scholars, scientists, and philosophers. Avicenna was one of them. Born in Persia in 980, he was the personal physician to more than one sovereign, but importantly he was also a philosopher and theologian. Those of you who have difficulty studying philosophy, take heart: by his own admission Avicenna read Aristotle's *Metaphysics* forty times without understanding it. Eventually he learned the text by heart and only then did its meaning come to him. It is said he celebrated this event by distributing lavish gifts to the poor. Averroes, another great Islamic Aristotelian, was born in Cordoba in 1126, less than a decade before Maimonides, who was also born in Cordoba. Eventually known in Aristotelian circles as "the Commentator," Averroes was to have his name perpetuated by an influential form of Renaissance philosophy known as "Latin Averroism." Although Averroes and Maimonides may have been tutored by some of the same masters, their interpretations of Aristotle differ significantly. St. Thomas was to call Averroes the corrupter of Aristotle.

3. Halbertal, *Maimonides: Life and Thought*, 365.

It may not be out of place to note that a contemporary of the two Cordoba giants is Abélard of Paris, undoubtedly the greatest logician of his day. Paris had the logical works of Aristotle but not his important philosophical works, such as the *Physics*, *Metaphysics*, and the *de Anima*. And then there was Héloïse, in the words of Josef Pieper (citing Étienne Gilson), "That 'wild little Frenchwoman' who as a girl of seventeen knew Latin, Greek, and Hebrew, and who entered a convent for love of Abélard, and recited the verses of the Roman poet Lucan while she took the veil." Pieper added, quoting Gilson, "Before anyone can claim to have found a formula defining the Middle Ages, he must first find a definition of Héloïse."[4] Some may have visited the magnificent tomb of Héloïse and Abélard in the Père-Lachaise Cemetery in Paris.

Maimonides was born into an Orthodox Jewish family and studied with his father and other masters in Cordoba. Before he reached the age of thirteen, his peaceful world was suddenly disturbed by the ravages of war and persecution when the political culture of Cordoba came under the dominance of the Almohads. As a result, the Jewish community, like the Christian, was faced with the choice between converting to Islam or leaving the city. The Maimon family temporized by practicing Judaism within the privacy of their home while disguising their ways in public. This double life proved irksome, and the family eventually fled in 1159 to Fez, Morocco, which turned out to be not

---

4. Josef Pieper, *Scholasticism: Personalities and Problems of Medieval Philosophy* (New York: Pantheon Books, 1960); citing Étienne Gilson, *Heloise et Abelard* (Paris: Librairie Philosophie, 1948). In the official English translation of Gilson's book, this quotation appears as: "Before attempting to define the Middle Ages, we should have first to define Héloïse." *Héloïse et Abélard*, trans. L. K. Shook (Chicago: Regnery Company, 1951), 143.

much better—forcing the family to move again—when in 1165 Rabbi Judah ibn Shoshan, with whom Moses was studying, was arrested as a practicing Jew and executed. Moses himself was denounced as reverting to Judaism after having embraced Islam. The penalty for reversion under the Almohads was death, but Moses managed to vindicate himself.

This turbulent background did not prevent Moses at age sixteen from composing a treatise on logic. The works to which we now attend were written in Egypt, where the family finally settled. But one further note: for the early part of his life, Maimonides was sustained by the family fortune. In 1177, tragedy struck when his younger brother David drowned in the Indian Ocean while on a trading mission. Maimonides, who would not take compensation as a rabbi, was obliged to establish a medical practice to support his family, which now included his brother's widow and child. Maimonides became renowned as a physician, and the oath he created for anyone who was about to practice medicine is still used as an alternative option to the more famous Hippocratic Oath.

Maimonides took fifteen years to write the *Guide for the Perplexed*. Its central thesis can be briefly stated: when science and philosophy conflict with Jewish tradition, the tradition itself is to be reinterpreted or reconciled with the truths of natural reason. The interpretation of Judaism that Maimonides offers is not meant solely to reconcile belief grounded in the *Torah* with the findings of philosophy and science but also to show that philosophy plays a central role in constructing the religious outlook itself. Knowledge independent of the tradition is also necessary for an understanding of the tradition. Without science and philosophy, we cannot tell whether a particular term or account in the *Torah* is to be taken literally or not. Furthermore, the pursuit of wisdom is a substantive part of the religious person's inner journey, vital to the redemption of his soul, especially in his moving from fear of God to love of God. The study of philosophy thus becomes for Maimonides a religious duty, for "to know, love and fear God" is man's highest duty, something that cannot be attained without the aid of wisdom. In fact, in the early chapters of the *Mishneh Torah* God is described in the metaphysical terms of essence and existence, not in descriptive personal or historical terms.

Whereas the *Mishneh Torah* is directed to a wide audience, elite and common folk alike, the *Guide for the Perplexed* is intended for a narrower group, people who have been educated to be faithful to the traditions of Judaism but who have also internalized the philosophical view of the world. In fact, the *Guide* conceals its deepest meaning from the reader who has not been initiated into philosophy. The perplexed, as defined by Maimonides, are confronted with two sources of authority, the *Torah* and wisdom. They are faced with what some might call an "existential crisis," a choice between religious faith and philosophical certainty. The *Guide* deliberately leaves the text open to multiple readings, that is, different interpretations of the *Torah*, depending on what the reader brings to the text. Four readings are possible. A skeptical reading, for one, sees philosophy as a critical tool, leading to the conclusion that no positive knowledge of God can be conveyed through language—thus, in effect, preserving God's pristine unity and transcendence, albeit in silence. A mystical reading looks upon philosophy as a process that clears the way to direct illumination, to a meta-linguistic, meta-rational experience of God.

Mystical experience takes place after one's consciousness is emptied of all positive content, especially through the negation of language. The mystical reading, unlike the skeptical, believes in a direct cognition—albeit a non-linguistic illumination—of

God. A third reading, the conservative reading, holds that the *Guide*'s greatest achievement lies in showing that the eternal preexistence of the world, as Aristotle would have it, cannot be proved. The perplexed person thus can adhere to the philosophical way without challenging the foundations of Judaism, which necessarily entails the ascription of will to God—for it is divine will that is exercised through creation ex nihilo, a cardinal tenet of the Hebrew Bible. A fourth reading, the philosophical reading, by contrast, maintains that the *Guide* provides a systematic interpretation of Judaism's fundamental concepts on the basis of wisdom and on the acknowledged reality of an eternal, preexisting world. These multiple ways of uncovering the hidden meaning of the *Torah* make it possible for the perplexed person to internalize the tradition of Greco-Arab philosophy without weakening his tie to Israel's *Torah*. It is important to keep in mind that for Maimonides there is no such thing as religious experience. All cognition or true belief arises from human intellect, sense perception, opinion, or tradition. Commentators, in keeping with Maimonides, acknowledge that there is no one way to understand the Jewish tradition.

It is in the context of his discussion of human perfection that Maimonides illustrates his doctrine of free will. He begins by noting that man alone among the creatures is granted free will. What distinguishes him from the brute is the ability to use his will to subject his desires and lusts to law and models of proper conduct. The practice of virtue is important not simply for its own sake but because it makes the intellectual life possible. The road to human perfection is attained only when will is in conformity to right reason. Fulfillment of the Commandments is a means, not an end. Put another way, intellectual acumen is possible only within the context of a well-ordered life. And here Maimonides draws a bit on Avicenna, who observed that man, as a social animal, cannot have a satisfactory life except within a political community. Tranquility is elusive given the inability of average men to create by their own unaided efforts a viable political society. When people are left to their own devices, they find it impossible to agree on a common law valid for all. Everyone thinks that the things that accord with his own interests are right and that the things that are unfavorable are wrong. Consequently, men are hostile to one another. Only a prophet, that is, a man endowed with certain faculties not found in the run of people, can create a social bond among them and thus preserve the community from calamities and self-destruction, leading them to submit to a law binding on all.

Maimonides, in keeping with his religious tradition, finds the end of life in the next world. Rather than being a reward for observing the Commandments, the world to come is a life devoted to the apprehension of the intelligibles for which this world is a preparation. Life in the world to come is thus a pure and refined continuation of the mind. From an Aristotelian point of view, human potential is fulfilled through apprehending to the full extent of one's intelligence truth about the world and God. According to Aristotle, in death, after one subtracts that which man has in common with plants (nutrition and growth) and with nonhuman animals (sensation), what remains is the distinctly human quality of intelligence. Put another way, what remains of a person after death is the knowledge he has acquired in this life. The immortality of the human soul from that point of view is no miracle; it simply follows causally from a certain way of life.

Given that human life attains its ultimate perfection through knowledge, all other human activity is subservient to this higher purpose. Because man is a material creature, he needs a well-ordered society that can provide him with the necessities required for the pursuit of a life of the mind. Thus, Maimonides can say that the observance of the Commandments, requiring or prohibiting various actions, is not the purpose of religion; it rather is the means by which man is to fulfill his purpose as a knowing creature.

Having addressed the problem of "creation in time," "life after death," and the "nature of morality," Maimonides was forced to address the problem of "free will." His is not the contemporary problem of "psychological determinism" or "genetic determinism," although the latter may be more ideology than science. He readily acknowledged the role of social pressures on individual action. It is natural, he believed, to be influenced in sentiment and conduct by neighbors and associates and by the observed customs of one's fellow citizens. The problem he faced in the *Guide* was how to reconcile human freedom with God's foreknowledge. If God knows from all eternity that you are going to run that Jaguar into a ditch, what freedom do you have? Seemingly your fate is sealed. But for Maimonides this is not a real problem. By definition, God exists outside of time. His knowledge does not interfere in the causal order ordained by the act of creation. Misfortune befalls the just and unjust alike. God does not intervene to free the just from poverty, illness, or travail. Although Aristotle held that the world is eternal, it is a derivative of Aristotelian teaching that enables Maimonides to understand divine providence.

Aristotle taught that the world has structure and order, but that structure does not determine the existence of each and every individual; rather, it is expressed in the maintenance of each species overall. Accordingly, the continuation of the animal species and humankind as a whole is ensured, but each individual is subject to random chance within the process of destruction and formation that governs his material nature. In Aristotle's view, providence does not connote God's willful involvement in a person's life or even in the history of a species or nation.

Maimonides adopts Aristotle's position: providence pertains to the species, not to individuals. Man is given the instruments of thought and movement that allow him to survive. In that sense, life is providential. It is not God's intervention from without; it is the wisdom that adheres in the causal order that, if mastered, makes existence and its preservation possible. Maimonides acknowledges that there are other schools of thought on the subject. The Ash'arites, for example, hold that providence is an ongoing volitional action on the part of God who controls all events in the universe. To Maimonides this position undermines the raison d'être of the Commandments. How can men be directed to observe the *Torah*'s Commandments if they are unable to observe them or transgress to the contrary.

Perhaps I should have mentioned in the beginning that Leo Strauss, in his preface to Shlomo Pines's translation of the *Guide*, warns the reader, "It is not a philosophical book: a book written by a philosopher for philosophers—but a Jewish book: written by a Jew for Jews."[5] Strauss will also say that the *Guide* contains a public teaching and a secret teaching. "The public teaching is addressed to every Jew, including the vulgar; the secret teaching is addressed to the elite. The secret teaching is of no use to the vulgar, and the elite does not need the *Guide* for being apprised of the public teaching."[6] One may beg to differ.

---

5. Leo Strauss, introductory essay to *The Guide of the Perplexed*, by Moses Maimonides, trans. Shlomo Pines (Chicago: University of Chicago Press, 1974), xiv.

6. Strauss, *Guide of the Perplexed*, xvi.

The public teaching may have been intended as such, but in my judgment, it is more than that, given its time-transcending value, a characteristic that makes the *Guide* a part of the Western literary canon. In appropriating Aristotle's metaphysics, Maimonides exemplifies the perennial value of the Stagirite as one grapples with problems that will not go away in spite of the empiricism that dominates contemporary intellectual discourse, that is, the relation of faith and reason, creation, morality and law, teleology in nature, and human nature and its perfection, to name only a few.

## ❧11❧
## *Thought*

THOUGHT WAS THE TITLE of a highly respected Fordham University quarterly, published from 1926 to 1992. During that period, its website tells us, it published 267 issues containing over 5,000 English language contributions by philosophers, theologians, literary intellectuals, and others. Among its well-known contributors were Dietrich von Hildebrand, Bernard Lonergan, Jacques Maritain, Walker Percy, and Karl Rahner.

The journal was named appropriately, for it carried essays that could not be classified strictly as theology or philosophy in spite of their subject matter, and others that fell short of the scholarly apparatus demanded by technical journals such as *The Modern Schoolman* or *Speculum*. As a student, I valued my subscription and many years later I was sad to see the periodical go, although I was never a contributor.

In *The Legend of the Middle Ages*, Rémi Brague notes, "There are in history highly respectable works that one would never call philosophical, but for which vaguer terms such as 'wisdom literature' or 'thoughts' would be more appropriate."[1] He finds reinforcement for this judgment by reminding the reader that Heidegger places "thought" on a higher plane than philosophy. Brague is particularly sensitive to the broad cultural context in which philosophy in any period develops. He finds that philosophy generally develops in the light of opinions generally

---

1. Rémi Brague, *The Legend of the Middle Ages: Philosophical Explorations of Medieval Christianity, Judaism, and Islam*, trans. Lydia G. Cochrane (Chicago: University of Chicago Press, 2009), 47.

admitted within a given community. The Arab world, as Brague notes, makes room for something between Falsafa (philosophy) and Kalam (theology). The problem is how much credibility is to be assigned to thought or "true opinion," as in Plato. Absent demonstration, can we acknowledge truth?

Plato in the *Meno*, after introducing the notion of "true opinion," has Socrates speak of the value of such knowledge. True opinion, although supported by fact, falls short of demonstrative knowledge, but is nevertheless required by him who would govern. "Men," says Socrates, "become good and useful to the state, not only because they have knowledge, but because they have right opinion."[2]

Pope Benedict XVI said much the same thing in an address he gave to the World Culture meeting in Venice in 2011. Rejecting the notion that European culture is "liquid," Benedict affirmed that judgment in matters of culture and economics depends not only on one's assessment of the present but largely on one's historical insight. He recognized that any argument based on history falls short of demonstration, yet knowledge of history enhances one's ability to make informed judgments. "Men and women are free to interpret and give meaning to reality, and it is in this freedom itself that the great dignity of the human being consists," he said, but in doing so they "must not be afraid . . . of the Gospel," aware of the tendency on the part of the European intellectual elite to ignore the Christian sources of Western culture as they advance their progressive agenda.[3]

Anyone who has followed the lectures and essays of Joseph Ratzinger from his years as professor of theology in Regensburg

---

2. Plato, *Meno*, 98c.
3. Benedict XVI, "Address to the Meeting with Representatives from the Worlds of Culture and the Economy (Venice)," May 8, 2011.

to his discourse as Pope Emeritus, or "Father Ratzinger," as he prefers to be addressed, will find in them a wisdom—"true opinion," one may say, rooted in both scholarship and experience. His is the type of knowledge that Plato prescribed for him who would govern.

To return to my theme, much of Professor Ratzinger's work could have been published in *Thought*, but one will not find it there. One will find it instead in *Communio*, a journal he founded with Hans Urs von Balthasar and Henri de Lubac in 1972 shortly after he became professor of theology at Regensburg.

## ❧12❧
# Lee Congdon on Russia

LEE CONGDON ADDRESSES a continuing theme of this volume in his *Solzhenitsyn: The Historical-Spiritual Destinies of Russia and the West*. This book is descriptive of the prophetic voice of Aleksandr Solzhenitsyn (1918–2008), who was convinced that the West "had set out on a road similar to that which had led his own country into the abyss."[1] Solzhenitsyn first came to the attention of the Western literati in 1962 with the publication of *One Day in the Life of Ivan Denisovich*, the only book he was allowed to publish while in the Soviet Union. That was followed years later by his acclaimed *Gulag Archipelago*. In 1970 he was awarded the Nobel Prize for literature "for the ethical force with which he has pursued the indispensable traditions of Russian literature."[2]

In telling his story, Lee Congdon points out that Russia never experienced the Renaissance or the Reformation. What sets Russia apart from the West is her Orthodox Faith. It defines her sense of nation, history, and identity. "When men forget God, Solzhenitsyn believed, communism or a similar catastrophe is likely to be the fate that awaits them."[3] In 1973, he wrote a *Letter to Soviet Leaders* and sent a personal copy to Leonid Brezhnev, in which he challenged his countryman. "Could the Soviet leader not see that it was ideology, the

---

1. Lee Congdon, *Solzhenitsyn: The Historical-Spiritual Destinies of Russia and the West* (DeKalb, Ill.: Northern Illinois University Press, 2017), x.
2. Quoted in Congdon, 70.
3. Congdon, x.

Progressive World View, that led the regime to act in ways contrary to the interests of Russia and her people?"[4] He told Brezhnev that Christianity was "the only living spiritual force capable of undertaking the spiritual healing of Russia."[5] Brezhnev apparently read the letter, but dismissed it as "nonsense."[6] Solzhenitsyn was soon living in exile in the West, after the manuscript of *The Gulag Archipelago* was discovered by the KGB.

The Western left was appalled when it discovered that Solzhenitsyn in his defense of the Old Believers was not merely a nominal Christian but a committed Orthodox Christian. The Old Believers were followers of Archpriest Avvakum who refused to accept the seventeenth century reform of Orthodox texts and ritual. Although he did not have a favorable opinion of the Church hierarchy, Solzhenitsyn expressed admiration for the courage and faith of a humble parish priest and the Russian faithful to whom he administered. Congdon explains, "There were many reasons for Solzhenitsyn's defense of the Old Believers, including their political conservativism, opposition to Western influence and readiness to flee the 'permissive, disorder, and lack of religious piety, that they encountered in the densely populated urban areas.'"[7]

From Frankfurt, Solzhenitsyn in 1975 visited Paris, where he was heralded as a great and prophetic writer. Later, he trav-

---

4. Congdon, 71.

5. Solzhenitsyn, *Letter to Soviet Leaders*, trans. Hilary Sternberg (New York: Harper and Row, 1974), 57. Quoted in Congdon, 71n93.

6. Michael Scammell, ed., *The Solzhenitsyn Files*, trans. Catherine A. Fitzpatrick et al. (Chicago: Edition Q, 1995), 257. Quoted in Congdon, 71n94.

7. Congdon, 75. Quotation is from Roy R. Robson, *Old Believers in Modern Russia* (DeKalb, Ill.: Northern Illinois University Press, 1995), 23.

eled to North America, first visiting British Colombia and Alaska which, Congdon reports, "appealed because of its harsh climate and because it was formerly a Russian possession." Then too, "it was in Alaska that the Russian Orthodox first evangelized the native populations of North America."[8] His journey down the Pacific coast took him next to Stanford, where the Hoover Institution made him an honorary fellow. June 30 finds him in Washington, D.C., where speaking to members of the AFL-CIO, he told them that in their dealing with Soviet leaders they should be aware that "Soviet leaders respected only firmness and held in contempt those who constantly gave in to them."[9] Otherwise, his message was the same, Congdon relates: "The West might soon be faced with a fate similar to that experienced by Russia."[10] Returning to Europe in 1976, he gave an interview to BBC in March of that year. On the radio Solzhenitsyn told his listeners that he did not regard the West as a model for post-Communist Russia. England, he reminded his audience, had "forced the repatriation of 100,000 Soviet citizens at the close of World War II, most of whom Stalin put to death." At Nuremberg, he maintained, British and Western elites, "exhibited an inexplicable sympathy for revolutionaries and terrorists and a contempt for any reference to spiritual regeneration."[11]

He then added this piece of advice: "We the oppressed peoples of Russia, the oppressed peoples of Eastern Europe, watch with anguish the tragic enfeeblement of Europe. We offer you the experience of our suffering; we would like you to accept

8. Congdon, 75.
9. Congdon, 76.
10. Congdon, 76.
11. Congdon, 76.

it without paying the monstrous price of death and slavery that we have paid."[12]

In Spain, he had good words for the authoritarian rule of General Francisco Franco's government in comparison with the totalitarian Soviet Union. Needless to say, the world press "subjected his remarks to endless criticism."[13] When in 1976 it came to choosing a place to rest, he chose Vermont for a home. Invited to give Harvard University's Commencement Address in 1978, he spoke of the West's spiritual exhaustion. Congdon summarizes his message: "So obsessed was the West with 'human rights,' Solzhenitsyn noted, that it had forgotten human obligation. Its freedom had degenerated into license, its 'media' filled minds and souls with gossip and nonsense, its popular culture served only to coarsen and degrade, its people exhibited an unthinking sympathy for socialism, and its excessive rationalism and philosophical materialism which undermined their ability to recognize evil, and destroyed the habit of spiritual reflection."[14] Solzhenitsyn concludes, "We have placed too much hope in politics and social reform, only to find that we were being deprived of our most precious possession : our spiritual life."[15] As he told the AFL-CIO, Westerners may say, "It will never happen here. This will never come to us. It is not possible here." Solzhenitsyn responds, "It can happen. It is

---

12. Solzhenitsyn, *Warning to the West*, trans. Harris L. Coulter and Nataly Martin, ed. Alexis Kimoff (New York: Farrar, Strauss and Giroux, 1976), 144. Quoted in Congdon, 77.

13. Congdon, 77.

14 Congdon, 78.

15. Solzhenitsyn in *Solzhenitsyn at Harvard*, ed. Ronald Berman (Washington, D.C,: Ethics and Public Policy Center, 1980), 12, quoted in Congdon, 78.

possible. As an old Russian proverb says, 'When it happens to you, you will know it is true.'"[16]

One must applaud Lee Congdon, emeritus professor of history, James Madison University, for this timely volume. It follows several of his acclaimed books: *Exiled Social Thought*, *Seeing Red*, and *George Kennan: A Writing Life*. He also co-edited a two-volume work on the Hungarian Revolution.

---

16. Solzhenitsyn, *Warning to the West*, 53. Quoted in Congdon, 76.

## ≈13≈
# The Concept of Person

IN A SENSE there is no such thing as American legal theory. Like science, theory transcends national boundaries. The legal theory in the United States has deep roots in classical and medieval philosophy and more immediately in the British common law. To seek the roots of the current legal meaning of "person" is to open the history of Western political thought, for it is the political theory of a given period that gives flesh to the term.

In fact, the Greek and Roman sources of the Western concept of person are well-known. Boethius's famous definition has been repeated ever since the sixth century, when in the context of a discussion of the Trinity he defined person, using Aristotelian terminology, as "a supposit of a rational nature." Throughout most of Western history, discussions of the concept of person have usually taken place within a philosophical or theological context. This remained unchanged until the twentieth century, when a shift occurred from the ontological to the psychological—a shift reflected in the dicta of the courts as they began to place more confidence in psychology and the social science than in philosophical discussion. Given this sequence of events, to approach the topic historically is to approach it metaphysically, though only up to a point. Which perspective is taken, psychological or metaphysical, makes a great deal of difference.

At least five different usages of the term "person" can be detected in American legal theory. The first arises in discussions of justice, since persons are obviously the locus of rights and duties. The second is found in property law, where the right to possession depends on an expanded notion of person. The third appears as the notion of person is extended to the corporation. The fourth arises historically in debates concerning the legal right of the slave. And the fifth arises in the context of *Roe v. Wade*, which overturned statutes in Texas and Georgia prohibiting abortion.

Alasdair MacIntyre, in a book that has become something of a modern classic—*Whose Justice, Which Rationality?*—has shown the difference a perspective can make. Émile Durkheim and Auguste Comte, who stand at the birth of social science and psychology, were both empiricists in the mold of David Hume. As MacIntyre has shown clearly, one can be a disciple of David Hume or of Aristotle, but one cannot be a disciple of both. Furthermore, one cannot be either without appropriate social organizations or without a congenial polis.

In 1962, Lord Patrick Devlin reminded his countrymen that if the morals of the community change, the laws will change too. He showed that the concept of "person" cannot be merely technical or legal. Concepts of person are grounded in considerations of human nature, in the belief of the absolute moral worth of the human being, in the spiritual equality of individuals, and in the essential rationality of man. These concepts are all a legacy from the Middle Ages, with roots deep in Greek and early Christian thought. Repudiation of this legacy would entail the repudiation of much of British common law, and the same could be said of other Western nations.

In the United States common law is grounded in the belief in the absolute moral worth of the person that prevents the individual from being submerged—if not obliterated—in a conception of race, class, national origin, or some other collectivity that regards the individual as a means rather than an end. This is reflected in discussions of justice that make a basic distinction between what an individual owes to other individuals by virtue of contractual obligation, and what he owes his community by virtue of the benefits he enjoys through membership.

Recognition of personal autonomy is the ultimate grounding of one's legal standing, that is, of what ought to be acknowledged or respected by others and protected by the law. "Autonomy" means that a person can never become a mere means for the community. The American Republic was founded on the assumption that the state has the obligation to safeguard rights which it recognizes but does not confer. No matter how rights are conceived or how numerous they are proclaimed to be, they arise as claims against the positive or civil law. They are presented as personal entitlements that the community, though it may have the power to do so, is not free to abrogate. The recognition of rights follows upon a natural law concept of person and a judgment of what leads to personal fulfillment.

Today, intellectual elites war against the principles on which the United States Constitution was founded. We hear arguments under the influence of Durkheim's social theory that claim a person must be thought of as a social production. Some authors claim that to be considered a person one must be socially defined, a publicly visible embodied being, endowed with powers and capacities for public meaningful action. This obviously excludes the child in utero. Such a definition contrasts sharply with the notion of person embodied in American law until *Roe v Wade*.

For Durkheim, crime is to be understood as a serious affront against the "collective experience," that is, the common morality that holds men together when sentiment is strong and precise. The collective conscience need not be correct or dictated by any natural law. It is sufficient that the value it promotes be held strongly by the community.

One can give a list of cases where a common-sense notion of person was accepted in American courts. Most often "person" was defined for legal purposes as a human being, distinguished from a thing or a lower animal. Courts commonly recognized that an unborn child falls within the meaning of person. To cite one example, the Kentucky Court of Appeals in *Mitchell v. Couch* found on behalf of the child *en ventra* if it sustained harm as a result of negligent injury done to his mother. The Court said in its 1855 opinion: "A viable unborn child is an entity within the general meaning of the word 'person' because biologically speaking the child is a presently existing person, a living human being."[1] From an empiricist point of view such a ruling would have been impossible.

The question to be confronted is whether empiricism, the philosophical materialism of Durkheim and Comte and their successors, can support biblical morality and the law we have known. Social conscience takes a hundred and eighty degree turn when empiricism is affirmed and the metaphysical is denied. Under such a construction there are no rights anterior to law and no rights contrary to law. The implications for tort and contract law are enormous. Attribution of blame may be given without causal evidence. One generation may be held accountable for the deeds of another. "Retribution," it is called. Changing attitudes among legal theorists and decades of judicial activism have not only made tort litigation a risky business for industry but have altered the traditional role of law in society and have obfuscated the purpose of law in general.

There is nothing new here. All of this is well-known, but given present social conflict and current political debate as I write, a few basic principles and facts are worth recalling. It is

---

1. *Mitchell v. Couch*, 285 S.W.2d 901 (Ky. Ct. App. 1955).

commonly acknowledged that candidates for office will say almost anything to appeal to their "base"—that group of people willing to spend time, money, and energy to secure their candidate's election. Currently the "base" for one of the parties appears to consist of individuals who recognize "persons with rights" only insofar as they challenge the majority of society. We find lists of things that must be done for the mosaic minority by the majority whose own rights are utterly discounted. Not even Durkheim would have gone that far.

# ❧14❦
# Purity in Aspiration

THROUGHOUT THE NINETEENTH and most of the twentieth century, schoolbooks depicted the early European settlers of the North American Continent as noble-minded immigrants, persecuted in the Old World for their religious faith and bent on the creation of a more congenial society in the New. In spite of attempts to totally secularize public school curricula, that story may yet prevail, if only to support the liberal immigration policy advanced by the progressive left. The truth is far more interesting, and, perhaps more relevant.

From the ranks of the Pilgrims who settled in the New World between 1620 and 1630 emerged a theocracy that was to prevail in the New England through the latter part of the seventeenth century and most of the eighteenth. It was a theocracy that came to be replaced by a democracy in accord with its own conception of God's plan for mankind. The Puritans were a reform-minded group in the Anglican Church whose objective was the practice of Christianity in its pristine purity. Opposed to what they described as "fleshly and worldly compromise," opposed to sacramental ritual and all rite, the Puritans insisted in doctrinal matters on the "right of private judgment" and in worship on the "priesthood of all believers." They were united in their conviction that the Church of England had not gone far enough in disassociating itself from the Church of Rome.

The most renowned congregation of Puritans is the one that fled Holland in 1607, sailing from Scrooby, Holland, on the Mayflower to the shores of Cape Cod where the Plymouth

Colony was established in 1620. That colony became the model for many others in North America. Taking their cue from Thomas Cartwright, the Puritan Bay Colony fashioned a framework for the Church. Only the elect would vote and rule in the commonwealth. The Church was not to govern, but it was to supply the instruments of rule, namely, the rationale for law and the principles that determine election procedures. "Biblical law was the primary law for the ordering of both church and state."[1] The Bay Colony prospered, and it was taken as evidence of the favor of God. True, it had its heretics, Roger Williams, Anne Hutchison, and Mary Dyer, for example, and the Colony did not hesitate to banish them. Some among the banished Quaker group founded by Dyer returned, only to be punished and finally hanged.

No colony escaped Puritan influence, not even the colony named after William Penn. It has been estimated that eighty-five per cent of the churches in the original thirteen colonies were Puritan in spirit. Calvin eventually became their most important theologian. Purifying worship became a major objective. Ritual and symbol were replaced by preaching, prayer, and the singing of psalms. Sermons based on biblical texts could last from one to two hours, not only on Sundays but on market days as well. Congregations were divided on whether to legislate for the community as a whole; overcoming difference, the famous New England "blue laws" came into being. They were the result of the Puritan effort to enforce community-wide observance of the Ten Commandments.

Because the preaching of the word of God was paramount in importance, ministers required superior education. Their

---

1. *New Encyclopedia Brittanica: Macropedia*, 19 vol. (Chicago: Encyclopedia Brittanica, 1983), 307.

training grounds were the New England grammar schools and seminaries, modeled on the English, and they became the foundation for some of the country's most distinguished schools. Institutions that we know today as the Boston Latin School and Harvard College were established within ten years of the landing of the Bay Colony.

The North American shores attracted not only the Puritans but also a multiplicity of other dissenting religious groups. By the time of the American Revolution and the framing of the United States Constitution, it was clear that no one religious group was dominant. The compromise worked out by the Constitutional Convention repudiated a national church but allowed each state among the original thirteen to determine its official church. It was not until the early decades of the nineteenth century that it became clear that there could not be, even at the state level, an official church. Although Virginia disestablished the Church of England in 1786, Connecticut did not disestablish the Congregation Church until 1818.

With independence, the spokesmen for the colonists still took for granted the good effects of religion as they drafted the federal and state constitutions. The problem at hand was the adjudication of the conflict among a multiplicity of sects. George Mason's draft of the Virginia Declaration of Rights provided that men should enjoy "the fullest toleration in the exercise of religion."[2] His colleague, James Madison, thought that stronger language was needed since toleration could be taken to mean only a limited form of religious liberty, that is, toleration of dissenters in a state where there was an established

2. George Mason, first draft of the Virginia Declaration of Rights, available at https://gunstonhall.org/learn/george-mason/virginia-declaration-of-rights/virginia-declaration-of-rights-first-draft/

church. Madison drafted a substitute, declaring that "all men are equally entitled to a full exercise of religion," and, therefore "no man or class of men, on account of religion, be invested with any peculiar emolument or privileges."[3] Madison was writing in a state that did in fact have an established church, and it was not his intent to disestablish the Anglican Church in Virginia. Out of the Virginia debate came the First Amendment of the U.S. Constitution with its declaration that "Congress shall make no law respecting an establishment of religion or preventing the free exercise thereof."[4]

The neutrality doctrine which governed legislation in the early days of the Republic eventually came to be construed by the United States Supreme Court as neutrality between religion and irreligion. Such a turn may have surprised Thomas Jefferson who, while he spoke of a "wall of separation," never wanted to divorce religion from public life. The founders of modern political theory like Thomas Hobbes and John Locke believed in the social utility of religion. John Stuart Mill repudiated Christianity but not the "religion of humanity."[5] Auguste Comte, in spite of his denial of all metaphysical validity of religious belief, was willing to accept as a civic good the moral and ritual traditions of at least Catholic Christianity.[6] Émile Durkheim was not so positive. For him the major task of the state was to free individuals from partial societies such

    3. *The Papers of James Madison*, ed. William T. Hutchinson and William M. E. Rachals (Chicago: University of Chicago Press, 1962), vol. 1, 174.

    4. U.S. Const. amend. I.

    5. John Stuart Mill, *Nature and Utility of Religion* (New York: The Liberal Arts Press, 1958).

    6. Auguste Comte, "Plan of the Scientific Operations Necessary for Reorganizing Society," *On Intellectuals,* ed. Philip Rieff (Garden City, NY: Doubleday, 1969).

as families, religious collectives, and labor and professional groups.[7]

In the twentieth century, John Dewey was to adopt the views of Mill and Durkheim. Whereas Dewey began his career speaking of "our obligation to know God,"[8] the mature Dewey had no use for religious institutions, whatever roles they may have played in the past. Religion, he held, is an unreliable source of knowledge and, in spite of contentions to the contrary, even of motivation. The thrust of Dewey's critique of religion was not merely to eliminate churches from political life but to reduce their effectiveness as agencies in private life. Dewey's philosophy became, de facto, that of the American public school, with consequences for morality and culture.

As Europe cedes the Continent to Islam, we may be aware but reluctant to accept the pessimism of prominent political theorists who try to envision what life might be like under an Islamic theocracy at odds with Christianity. We in the United States are beginning to face a similar fate as our institutions come under the influence of an intellectual cadre at war with Christianity. Absent a respect for the Constitution's Bill of Rights, absent the recognition of a natural moral law, all decisions become political. Unless the Constitution holds, those who control the media are apt to determine the future of the country.

---

7. Émile Durkheim, *The Elementary Forms of Religious Life*, trans. J. W. Swain (New York: Collier, 1961).

8. John Dewey, "The Obligation to Knowledge of God," in *The Collected Works of John Dewey, 1882–1953*, ed. Jo A. Boydston, vol. 1 (Carbondale: Southern Illinois University Press, 1967), 61.

# Part III

# ⁂15⁂
# Rémi Brague

IN 2011, Rémi Brague occupied the prestigious Cardinal Mercier Chair of Philosophy at the Catholic University of Louvain, where he gave a series of lectures that are relevant to the theme of this book. Reflections initiated there were further developed in subsequent works, *Eccentric Culture* (2012) and *On the God of the Christians and One or Two Others* (2013). The focus of these works is the character of European civilization, its formation, development, and challenges. "European culture," the translator Paul Seaton declares, "was formed by Christianity, the religion of the Creative Logos, and its fraught but fruitful engagement with the philosophical logos of antiquity."[1] Today that culture is on the defensive. What took centuries to construct has taken only a few decades to contest. Given the present schizophrenia that seems to characterize European intellectuals, Brague finds it necessary to state what and who man is and his difference from the rest of nature.

Man is understood as constituting a species distinguished from others by certain properties he possesses exclusively. He is a rational animal, a social animal, a political animal, superior to all other living beings.[2] He is cognizant of the intention of nature. "Nature, it may be said, "glorifies herself in him."[3]

---

1. Rémi Brague, *The Legitimacy of the Human*, trans. Paul Seaton (South Bend, Ind.: St. Augustine's Press, 2018), viii.
2. Aristotle, *Nicomachean Ethics*, VI, 7, 1141a34–1141b1, cited in Brague, *The Legitimacy of the Human*, 6.
3. Brague, *The Legitimacy of the Human*, 7.

"Moreover, his status as the greatest success of nature assures him proximity to the divine."[4] Man also realizes his superiority in his conquest of nature. Francis Bacon spoke of the *regunum hominis*,"[5] and René Descartes of "the master and possessor of nature."[6] But the dominion of man over the rest of things has not gone without saying. In antiquity Brague finds Pythagoras and Porphyry promoting questionable accounts of the nature in man. Modern natural science similarly is often guilty of ignoring the unique status of the human being. Biologists have said that the human species is "a deviation of nature"—a *faux pas*, as Max Scheler put it.[7] From that viewpoint the very existence of man is taken as a danger to other species.

Brague reminds his readers that those engaged in the natural sciences do not deal with the human as such. "The science of nature in its modern version is . . . a dehumanizing authority."[8] We falsely expect the improvement of the human condition by means of a scientific increase in our knowledge of the nonhuman. But in the modern study of nature one finds no trace of human values. "Science refuses to answer the question posed by man,"[9] namely the question of purpose or the final cause of nature and human nature. The scientist is forbidden

---

4. Brague, 7.

5. Francis Bacon, *Novum Organum: Aphorismi de interpretatione naturae et regno hominis*, ed. W. Krohn (Darmstadt: Wissenschaftlich Buchgesellschaft, 1990), 80, 144, cited in Brague, *The Legitimacy of the Human*, 9.

6. René Descartes, *Discours de la méthode*, VI, in *Ouevres*, ed. Ch. Adam and P. Tannery (Paris: Leopold Cerf, 1902), t. VI, 61–62, cited in Brague, *The Legitimacy of the Human*, 9.

7. Brague, *The Legitimacy of the Human*, 45, citing M. Scheler, *Schriften zur Anthropologie*, ed. M. Arndt (Stuttgart: Reclam, 1994), 46, 55, and 63.

8. Brague, *The Legitimacy of the Human*, 27.

9. Brague, *The Legitimacy of the Human*, 28.

to ask *why*. He is confined to description and the formulation of laws. "The motto of modern science is fundamentally the same rule that governs the conduct of inferiors vis-à-vis their superiors in the army: 'no need to understand!'"[10] "As needed," the scientist may seek "the complicitous aid of philosophers, who will explain that" those *why* questions "are meaningless."[11]

We turn to the "humanities" for correction, but more and more the humanities are eclipsed by the exact sciences. The term "humanities" itself dates to antiquity. Ever since Cicero, the type of learning he called *humaniora* has entailed "the study of good authors."[12] 'The classics,' we call them now. They were "thought to render one who devoted him- or herself to them 'more human' (*humanior*)."[13] We speak of Renaissance humanism. In the nineteen century, the Weimar authors, Goethe and Schiller, came to be regarded as "the foremost representatives of humanism."[14]

Following the order of his Mercier lectures, Brague devotes a chapter to the thought of Alexander Blok (1880–1921), the Russian poet. Another chapter is devoted to Michel Foucault (1926–1984), the French philosopher and historian, and yet another to Hans Blumenberg's book, *The Legitimacy of the Modern*.

"Modern times" Brague observes, "understand themselves as a rupture vis-à-vis the preceding period," not simply as something that is "more recent than that which preceded it," but as something that "tore itself decisively away from a past in

10. Brague, 28.
11. Brague, 28.
12. Brague, 24.
13. Brague, 24.
14. Brague, 78.

order to establish itself irrevocably in its own, and definitive, reality."[15] The "transition to Modernity was not simply undergone, but consciously willed."[16] "To be modern," Brague insists, "is to want to be modern and to know one's self as such."[17] "The passage to Modernity is a choice"—a repudiation of the past—"a rupture in the unbroken continuity of history."[18] If we attempt to define it, its description would contain reference to the conquest of nature, application of mathematical physics, and technology that gives control. But one cannot live by modern science alone.

A return to the perspective of the Middle Ages is, Brague insists, "inevitable," but "the real question is to know *what sort of Middle Ages* we would wish, or rather: what sort *ought* to desire to return"?[19] Not one, Brague claims, devoid of modern industrial achievements or devoid of contemporary medicine. Alfred Loisy is quoted as saying, "[Early Christians may have] expected the Kingdom of God but it was the Church that came."[20] The Middle Ages conceived man as a creature of God. The subject of origins, says Brague, "has to be raised anew. One has to ask again: What made or marks man? Who or what deserves to be called his creator?"[21]

Distinguishing between "the idea of creation and 'creationism,' which rests on a naïvely literal reading of Genesis,"[22]

15. Brague, 113.
16. Brague, 113.
17. Brague, 113.
18. Brague, 113.
19. Brague, 132.
20. Alfred Loisy, *L'évangile et l'église* (Bellevue: Chez l'auteur, 1904.), 155. Cited in Brague, *The Legitimacy of the Human*, 125.
21. Brague, *The Legitimacy of the Human*, 134.
22. Brague, 143.

Brague finds inspiration in the biblical narrative that tells us that God looked upon His creation and found that it was good—thus attesting to "the *value* of what exists."[23] The natural sciences may describe reality, but it is not theirs to say that it is good or bad. Much of this perspective is affirmed in the May 2017 Paris Declaration, "A Europe We Can Believe In," signed by thirteen prominent European intellectuals, including Rémi Brague, Pierre Manent, and Robert Spaemann.

---

23. Brague, 143.

## ~16~
# Yemima Ben-Menahem

YEMIMA BEN-MENAHEM, writing in her *Causation in Science*, shows clearly that conceptions of scientific explanation have implications in the social order at all levels, including geopolitics. Ben-Menahem is professor of philosophy at the Hebrew University of Jerusalem. She is the author of *Conventionalism: From Poincaré to Quine*, editor of *Hilary Putnam*, and co-editor of *Probability in Physics*. The book begins with an account of the linguistic turn in the twentieth century, namely its shift from traditional philosophical enquiry to one that led philosophers to focus on the meaning of certain core concepts, such as causation, explanation, virtue, and liberty.

Ben-Menahem works from a realistic perspective, not quite Aristotelian, but headed that way. Her first task is to provide a definition of "causality." Causality, of course, is not directly observable. Rejecting David Hume's account of causality—as well as all empiricist accounts of causality—she notes that regularities, even when they appear to be law-like, may reflect accidental rather than causal connections. She insists that in distinguishing between laws and mere regularities, one must display a connection between the supposed cause and the concrete mechanism that facilitates it. She takes issue with Bertram Russell and J. D. Norton, who sought to banish the notion of cause from fundamental physics.

Ben-Menahem is led subsequently to a discussion of causal constraints—general constraints on change. The notion of causal constraint, she finds, is broader than the notion of cause.

Causal constraints must be distinguished from purely mathematical constraints, which are indifferent to temporal change and temporal evolution. A key goal of the scientific enterprise, she reminds the reader, is to explain not only that which occurs but that which is excluded from occurring. Put another way, "science seeks to identify constraints that distinguish what may happen, or what is bound to happen, from what is excluded from happening."[1]

An early chapter examines the notion of stability as a distinct member of the causal family. Stability is not to be identified as determinate. After examining the concept of cause in daily discourse, Ben-Menahem turns to the physical sciences. For the physicist, questions about the stability of states, orbits, and structures are fundamental. Stable structures, whether those of elementary particles, stars, or galaxies, are features of nature. Quantum mechanics, for example, had to face the question of the stability of atoms. Accounting for the atom's stability was one of the chief goals of quantum theory in the 1920s. Stability is also a central concept in other areas of physics such as thermodynamics and hydrodynamics. "Indeed, stability is integral to our understanding of change on every level of the physical world."[2] The stability of a state or dynamical orbit is characterized by its response to small perturbations. Important is the recognition that determinism and stability are independent notions. The deterministic laws of classical physics, Ben-Menahem finds, are compatible with both stable and unstable states and trajectories. Indeed, as Ben-Menahem shows in a later chapter, stability can be pred-

---

1. Yemima Ben-Menahem, *Causation in Science* (Princeton: Princeton University Press, 2018), 2.
2. Ben-Menahem, *Causation in Science*, 62.

icated of macro-phenomena when all systems at the micro level are equally unstable.

Newton was concerned with the stability of the solar system. The Indian astrophysicist Subrahmanyan Chandrasekhar is noted for pondering the stability of stars, wondering why they did not collapse under the inner force of their own gravity. Niels Bohr in 1939 produced a model of the atom based on an analogy of the solar system, with electromagnetic forces taking the place of gravity. Bohr soon realized, however, that according to classical electromagnetic theory electrons orbiting the nucleus would decrease continuously until they hit the nucleus. On this classical picture there could not be stable atoms. Bohr subsequently devised a quantum model according to which only discrete orbits—stationary states—are allowed, and further proposed that electrons in these stationary orbits do not lose energy through radiation. Ben-Menahem reports that this model was remarkably successful (in accounting for the data at hand).

A later chapter is devoted to a discussion of statistical mechanics and to an explanation of directionality. Statistical mechanics, a theory that pivots on questions of stability and directionality, is used to explain irreversibility. Ben-Menahem claims that more than a century of research has not produced a fully satisfactory explanation of what is called "the stability-directionality nexus." Classical thermodynamics was formulated in terms of macro-descriptions alone, whereas statistical mechanics seeks to connect the two levels (macro and micro) of description. This is followed by a discussion of the meaning of probability in statistical mechanics.

When speaking of entropy in statistical mechanics, Ben-Menahem finds that entropy is defined as the relation between macro and microstates. Recognizing the distinction between quantum mechanics and statistical mechanics, she finds that thermodynamics knows of no such notion as the entropy of a physical system.

The book is brought to a close by a discussion of the causal efficacy of mental events. The question at issue is whether mental events can be covered by the laws of fundamental physics. Ben-Menahem is convinced that "mental events of a certain kind do not constitute a corresponding physical type."[3] Given that the mental does not fit into the web of physical laws, Ben-Menahem is then led to review some familiar developments in twentieth century philosophy of mind. She devotes time to a discussion of Gilbert Ryle's *The Concept of Mind* and to the non-reductive physicalism of Donald Davidson and Hilary Putnam.

Without ignoring Yemima Ben-Menahem's many original insights, it must be said that *Causation in Science* provides a refreshing account of some ancient notions and distinctions known to those familiar with Aristotle's *Metaphysics*. More than that, by its focus on the first half of the twentieth century, the book recapitulates one of the most exciting periods in the history of theoretical physics. Anyone who possesses a college level knowledge of physics is likely to relive that period, given the author's informed account.

---

3. Ben-Menahem, 161.

## ❧17❧
## *On Human Worth and Excellence*

ONE DOES NOT HAVE TO BE a Renaissance historian or know much medieval philosophy or theology to appreciate Giannozzo Manetti's delightful book, *On Human Worth and Excellence*. The book was completed in 1452, less than a decade before the author's death in 1459 at the age of sixty-three. The book, for the first time, has recently been made available by the Harvard University Press.

It is just one of the many major literary, historical, philosophical, and scientific works of the Italian Renaissance that the press is reproducing in the English language from the I Tatti Renaissance Library. Beautifully produced, each volume provides a reliable Latin text together with a readable English translation on facing pages. The present work is graced by a splendid introduction written by Brian P. Copenhaver, the book's translator.

Manetti is not easy to classify—diplomat, classical scholar, biblical exegete, philosopher, theologian, natural scientist, his interests spanned all of those disciplines. A thoroughgoing Aristotelian, he venerated Cicero and Lactantius and drew heavily on the *Sentences* of Peter Lombard and contemporaries such as Bartolomeo Facio and Antonio da Barga. He translated Hebrew texts as well as Greek texts into Latin, notably the *History of Pistoria*, and produced books on the lives of Dante, Petrarch, Seneca, and Socrates.

He traces human worth to the nobility of the human soul. Some pagans, he notes, understood the special nature of the human soul. Aristotle spoke more clearly than Plato. He showed the soul to be "rational, immortal, and indestructible."[1] Cicero, taking his lead from Aristotle, in discussing the nature of the soul in the *Tusculan Disputations*, finds that the soul cannot be made but must be created. Add to that *Genesis*'s account of God's creation of the indestructible human soul from nothing, and you have a Christian anthropology.

*On Human Worth and Excellence* consists of four "books." Book I explores "human nature's perfect design,"[2] and with the aid of Cicero and Lactantius comes to the conclusion that "God so fashioned the human body as so splendid a marvel in order to form a worthy and also a fitting vessel for the rational soul."[3]

Book II then seeks a definition for the soul. Manetti is convinced that "the soul is a substance, an incorporeal form created by God out of nothing."[4] "Everything written in both Testaments, Old and New," he says, "presupposes this immortality of souls."[5] Manetti finds further support for this contention in the writings of Porphyry, Pythagoras, Seneca, and the Older Cyrus, whom he calls "the noblest Persian king."[6] If the soul is not immortal, he reasons, nature's desire and appetite for happiness could not be fulfilled. Manetti finds that Augustine in his analysis of the soul holds that its immateriality affirms man's creation in the likeness of God and proves mankind's superiority to the rest of creation. That rank, he thought, is con-

---

1. Giannozzo Manetti, *On Human Worth and Excellence*, ed. and trans. Brian P. Copenhaver (Cambridge, Mass.: Harvard University Press, 2019), 77.
2. Manetti, *On Human Worth and Excellence*, 9.
3. Manetti, 61.
4. Manetti, 87.
5. Manetti, 95.
6. Manetti, 93.

firmed when God "assigned each person a special angel from the moment of birth in order to guard them from wicked deeds and shameful acts."[7] But God gave his best gift when His only Son took on the lowly mortal body.

Book III is devoted to a discussion of the unity of body and soul. "Some extraordinary items belong to the body," Manetti says, "while others are remarkable and unique to the soul."[8] But there remains a few issues that need to be addressed concerning man's mortal existence. Some fail to see the work of divine providence when discussing the human being's origin. "Many, like Leucippus, Democritus and Epicurus, think the world was created by chance, while many Peripatetics think it has always existed, but the Stoics say that the world was formed and put in place by an all-powerful God."[9] Some ignore the beauty and pleasures of life that are part of God's providential plan. Life is not a shaky bridge over the chasm of hell as some imply. Stupidity and sin are not natural or essential features of human life. Man has the ability to manage and to govern the world that was made on his account. Manetti cites Lactantius's *The Divine Institutes* in support of his contention, "God made the world and set it up only for mankind's sake."[10]

Book IV begins: "I have brought together everything I found relevant to that special worth and singular excellence of man, everything important that bears on it."[11] The fourth book is largely a polemic against those who take a gloomy view of the

7. Manetti, 159.
8. Manetti, 117.
9. Manetti, 119.
10. Manetti, 123. The editor refers to the 7th chapter of *Divine Institutes* in his notes.
11. Manetti, 179.

human condition, those who focus on the misery and frailty of human life. A particular target is Lotario dei Segni (then a cardinal, later Innocent III), who produced in 1250 a book entitled, *On the Miseries of Human Life*. "Most people," Manetti insists, "rather than being racked by anguish and distress, are more taken with joys and pleasures" they experience in ordinary life, the enjoyment of eating and drinking.[12] They take pleasure in "warming up, cooling off and resting."[13] In an appendix, Manetti acknowledges the work of two contemporaries upon whom he has drawn: one by Antonio da Barga, *On Mankind's Worth and the Excellence of Human Life*, the other by Bartolomeo Facio, *On Human Excellence and Distinction*.

Manetti's knowledge of the ancients is astonishing, and, one may say, possessed by few today. Since the 1980s, magnetic resonance scanning has made the human brain visible in ways that have never been known before, but the human soul, which Manetti describes with the help of Aristotle and Cicero, will forever elude the modern-day Leucippus or Democritus.

---

12. Manetti, 205.
13. Manetti, 205.

## ༄18༅
# Reconstruction

"A GOTHIC CATHEDRAL is a collective achievement, the outcome of countless craftsmen working across the centuries toward a common goal. It is not the arena for idiosyncratic personal expression."[1] So wrote Michael J. Lewis in an essay, quoted in the preface to this volume. Something similar may be said of an intellectual tradition that was being formed at the same time the European cathedrals were coming into being.

Throughout this volume, our subject has been the formation of Western culture, the intellectual tools and the social conditions that contributed to its being. Stephen Gaukroger provides this insight. Like those great cathedrals, modern science is the outcome of a distinctive culture long in the making, a culture whose history begins in classical antiquity.[2] Specifically, what needs to be rebuilt in company with Notre Dame is a former Greek confidence in the human intellect, in its ability to reason to truths unseen, to truths that acknowledge the immaterial character of human intellection, the spiritual component of human nature. It takes a metaphysics and a realistic epistemology to facilitate such reasoning. But where is one to look for its revival? Reviewing contemporary philosophical literature, one might conclude that the primary objective of major university

---

1. Michael J. Lewis, "Rebuilding Notre Dame: Not So Fast," *Wall Street Journal*, May 1, 2019, https://www.wsj.com/articles/rebuilding-notre-dame-not-so-fast-11556744484.

2. See Stephen Gaukroger, *The Emergence of a Scientific Culture and the Shaping of Modernity 1210–1685* (Oxford: Clarendon Press, 2006).

presses today—given their endless production of brain and neural studies—is to reduce man to the status of a purely material organism. Other disciplines take their cue from what seems to be the latest biochemical research and take man's wholly material nature for granted. Alternative accounts of human nature are derided as faith-based or theologically derived.

In 1925, when Alfred North Whitehead delivered the Lowell Lectures at Harvard—lectures subsequently published as *Science and the Modern World*[3]—they were significant because they challenged the Enlightenment view that only with the repudiation of a religious world view could modern science have emerged from a dark age. Whitehead, it must be noted, was writing a generation before the in-depth studies of Marshall Clagett, A. C. Crombie, and Anneliese Maier, and before the monumental work of Pierre Duhem became available in the English-speaking world.

Examining the relation between science and culture, Whitehead put to himself a fundamental question: Why did modern science emerge in the West in the sixteenth and seventeenth centuries when all the conditions required for its birth were seemingly in place in classical antiquity? It was Whitehead's attempt to answer his own question that led him to examine the medieval and Renaissance background to modernity. Seven hundred years had elapsed between the fall of the Roman Empire and Newtonian physics. Whitehead's investigation led him to the conclusion that the Middle Ages prepared the way. "The Middle Ages," he wrote, "formed one long training of the intellect in Western Europe in the sense of order. There may have been some deficiency with respect to practice, but the idea

3. Alfred North Whitehead, *Science and the Modern World* (New York: Macmillan, 1925).

never for a moment lost its grip. It was predominantly an era of orderly thought, rational through and through."[4]

The habit of definite and exact thought Whitehead attributes to the Greek philosophers, but in the passage quoted he is less interested in the metaphysics that undergirds induction than he is in the reciprocal influence of theory and practice. "We owe it to St. Benedict," he writes, "that the monasteries were the homes of practical agriculturalists, as well as of saints and of artists and men of learning. The alliance of science with technology, by which learning is kept in contact with irreducible and stubborn facts, owes much to the practical bent of the early Benedictines."[5] Whitehead could cite monastic interest in medicine, in the improvement of farm instruments, in the harnessing of wind and waterpower, in mining, and in the promotion of crafts. A. C. Crombie records that by the eleventh century, some abbeys were to have as many as five water wheels, each powering a different shop. Thus, Whitehead draws the conclusion: "Modern science derives from Rome [Monte Cassino] as well as from Greece, and this Roman strain explains its gain in an energy of thought kept closely in contact with the world of facts."[6]

Lynn White Jr., a professor of history at the University of California at Los Angeles, picks up the theme in an essay entitled, "Dynamo and Virgin Reconsidered." This essay is but a prelude to his extensive study, *Medieval Technology and Social Change*. He offers a slightly different but compatible perspective, one that is also part of the present story. "The chief glory of the later Middle Ages," White says, "was not . . . its cathedrals,

4. Whitehead, 13.
5. Whitehead, 19.
6. Whitehead, 19.

its epics, its vast structures of scholastic philosophy . . . it was the building for the first time in history of a complex civilization which was upheld not on the sinews of sweating slaves and coolies but primarily by nonhuman power."[7] White goes on to say of the Benedictine that "the monk was the first intellectual in history to get dirt under his fingernail."[8] In the ancient world of Greece and Rome, manual work was the lot of the slave, whereas Benedict prescribed for his followers both work and prayer. In an agricultural society, that work entailed dirt under the fingernails or something similar. The significance of this we will attempt to show.

White's thesis is supported notably by two distinguished historians of science and culture, Pierre-Maxime Schuhl and Benjamin Farrington. Pierre-Maxime Schuhl wrote in the mid-decades of the twentieth century as chairman of the Sorbonne's philosophy department and as editor of the *Revue Philosophique*. Benjamin Farrington is known for his multiple works on Greek science. "Science," Farrington writes, "whatever its ultimate development, has its origins in techniques, in the arts, and crafts, in the various activities by which man keeps life going on. Its source is experience, its aims practical, its only test is that it works. Science derives from contact with things. It is dependent on the evidence of the senses. It requires logic and the elaboration of theory."[9] Finally, to understand science of any society is to be acquainted not only with its degree of material advancement but also with its political structure. "There is no such thing

---

7. Lynn White Jr., "Dynamo and Virgin Reconsidered," *The American Scholar* 27, no. 2 (1958): 192.

8. White, 189.

9. Benjamin Farrington, *Greek Science: Its Meaning for Us*, vol. 1, *Thales to Aristotle* (Harmondsworth, UK: Penguin, 1944), 14.

as science *in vacuo*," Farrington insists. "There is only the science of a particular place and time."[10] Farrington goes so far as to argue that the division of labor in Greek and Roman society retarded its development in the natural sciences.

Both Whitehead and Lynn White agree that from the decline of Roman civilization to the rise of European universities in the twelfth century, a period of 700 years, the Benedictine monasteries came to play an important role in the development of a Western science, both as bearers of classical learning and as cultivators in their own right of science and technology.

The story may begin at Monte Cassino, but one of Benedict's earliest disciples was Cassiodorus, one of the most learned men of his day. He lived from 490 to 585. Cassiodorus in advanced age was to found the monastery of Vivarium on the family estate at Squillace. As a classicist, Cassiodorus saw the need for the preservation of ancient texts from Greece and Rome, texts which formed the minds of Justin Martyr, Athenagoras, and Clement of Alexander—early Church Fathers—as they employed the texts of Plato, Aristotle, and the Stoics in their efforts to elucidate the teachings of the Gospels. With reason, Cassiodorus set his monks to the copying of those ancient texts. Though Benedict did not intend it, monasteries within his own lifetime became and were soon famous for their scriptoria, where the classics of antiquity were copied for posteriority.

By the thirteenth century there were more than 700 Benedictine monasteries spread across Europe. Some were to be numbered among the great cultural centers of Europe. Independent schools emerged in the abbeys, each seeking to outrival the other by increasing its library, by attracting professors of renown, and by drawing students to its intellectual tournaments.

10. Farrington, 15.

These schools promoted the sciences and were to create a legion of remarkable theologians, philosophers, and lawyers, as well as men of science. We need but cite the schools of Cluny, Cîteaux, Bec, Aurillac, St. Martin, and St. Omer. A roll call of the leading scholars of the age from Gregory through Bede, Lanfrank, and Anselm, would name the abbots of many of these monasteries. The twelfth century Benedictine abbot, Bernard of Clairvaux, became an author almost against his will. His books and monographs grew out of lectures recorded by his fellow monks who circulated them, sometimes without his knowledge, and often without his editorial scrutiny. A Brother Godfrey asked him to write about the virtue of humility and the result was *De Gradibus Humilitatis*. Thus did St. Bernard's works become part of our intellectual and spiritual heritage.

By the middle of the twelfth century the cathedral schools came to replace the monasteries as centers of learning and cultural influence. The introduction of Aristotle into the West in the twelfth and thirteenth centuries had an immediate and profound influence. In a sense it was a Greek revival, but more than that the European intellect had undergone a transformation between the Hellenist period and the advent of the medieval universities. If we were to compare the Christian attitude to the pursuit of knowledge—as exemplified in the Benedictine—with the previous Greek attitude, we would find not opposition but instead the Christian building upon the Greek. The Christian's conviction that nature is intelligible and directed toward ends is something he shares with his Greek predecessors. But in addition to that, he believes that God reveals Himself in Sacred Scripture, as well as in the book of nature.

What makes this relevant is that among the texts preserved in the monastic scripture were the *De Anima*, *Metaphysics*, and *Physics* of Aristotle, texts that were not previously available in the West. Those texts arrived contemporaneously with the building of the Cathedral of Notre Dame de Paris and formed the basis of an intellectual tradition that was to serve the West for centuries. We know it as "Scholasticism," the philosophy of Plato and Aristotle. In the twelfth century, it produced scholars of the rank of Averroes, Maimonides, Abelard, Anselm, and Hildegard of Bingen. In the thirteenth it produced Thomas Aquinas, Duns Scotus, Albertus Magnus, Robert Grosseteste, Roger Bacon, Bonaventure, and a host of others. That was not all that was going on. Historians tell us that around 1100 AD the economy of Europe increased dramatically, largely due to new techniques in the exploiting of wind and waterpower and in mining. Richard Lefebvre des Noëttes—a retired French military officer—as a result of extensive study and experimentation, attributes the great jump in part to the invention of the padded horse collar, which not only enabled the harnessing of horses in tandem but rendered a fourfold yield in the work of a properly shoed single horse. For the same amount of food necessary to maintain each, the power of a team of horses was increased substantially. Some have likened the surge in power to that experienced with the arrival of nuclear power in the twentieth century. Paul Gans provides an account in his study, "The Medieval Horse Harness: Revolution or Evolution."

These achievements are difficult to ignore, but no amount of scholarship will dispel the "dark age myth." It is part of a dogmatic package accepted on faith, sealed by willful ignorance. The world of Copernicus, Galileo, and Kepler knew better as Alfred North Whitehead was to discover.

## 19

*The Great Delusion*

*THE GREAT DELUSION* by John J. Mearsheimer, like Yemima Ben-Menaham, shows that conceptions of human nature have implications in the social order at all levels, including geopolitics. Mearsheimer is a political theorist and international relations scholar who holds the Wendell Harrison Distinguished Service Professorship at the University of Chicago. The book is an indictment of post-Cold War United States foreign policy. He tells us, "When I began working on this book ten years ago . . . I was interested in explaining why the post-Cold War U.S. foreign policy was so prone to failure, sometimes disastrous failure. I was especially interested in explaining America's fiascoes in the greater Middle East."[1] Mearsheimer finds that in the aftermath of the Cold War, the United States adopted a profoundly liberal foreign policy dedicated to turning as many countries as possible into liberal democracies, that is, to remake the world in its own image. It was driven by an idealistic assumption: 'The freedom we prize is not for us alone but is the right of all mankind.'

Unfortunately, in implementing that policy under Presidents George W. Bush and Barack Obama, Washington has played a key role in sowing death and destruction throughout the Middle East. Far from promoting cooperation and peace, liberal policy has brought instability and conflict.

---

1. John J. Mearsheimer, *The Great Delusion* (New Haven: Yale University Press, 2018), vii.

Exploring the foundations of liberalism, Mearsheimer contrasts liberalism and its assumptions with what he calls nationalism (the recognition that there are nations each with its own culture). First principles are important. It matters how one understands nature and human nature. Rhetorically, he asks, "Are men and women social beings above all else, or does it make more sense to emphasize their individuality?"[2] "Nation-states," he answers, "[reflect] the fact that human beings are principally social beings who have fundamentally different views on what constitutes the good life."[3] Liberalism plays down that social nature to the point of almost ignoring it by treating individuals as atomistic players. Furthermore, liberals ignore the geographic element which creates a social milieu that is foreign to others.

Jeremy Bentham may have called natural rights "rhetorical nonsense," but nationalists, embracing the concept of "natural rights," are skeptical of positive rights that can be both conferred and taken away by a rudderless state. Nationalists, perhaps better called realists, maintain that the state should involve itself as little as possible in personal and family life. In common, they resist government attempts at social engineering, in contrast to the liberal propensity to do so.

Mearsheimer presents himself as personally committed to liberal democracy. "I define democracy as a form of government with a broad franchise in which citizens get to choose their leaders in periodic elections. Those leaders then write and implement the rules that govern the polity. A liberal state privileges the rights of its citizens and protects them through its laws."[4]

2. Mearsheimer, 7.
3. Mearsheimer, 8.
4. Mearsheimer, 11.

Mearsheimer pursues his analysis under titles such as "The Limits and Perils of Social Engineering," "The Costs of Ignoring Geopolitics," and "Liberal Blindness." Mearsheimer shows that the liberal world view of the Bush and Obama administrations supported the expansion of the European Union and NATO into Eastern Europe. The United States and its allies, he finds, are mainly responsible for the ongoing crisis in the Ukraine. "The taproot of the trouble is NATO's expansion, and its larger strategy to move all of Eastern Europe, including Ukraine, out of Russia's orbit and integrate that territory into the West."[5]

George Kennan, historian and diplomat—who supported "containment policy" during the Cold War—after the collapse of the Soviet Union advised against the expansion of NATO to Russia's frontiers. In a 1998 interview, as quoted by Mearsheimer, he said: "I think it is a tragic mistake. There is no reason for it whatsoever. No one is threatening anyone else."[6] In short, in Mearsheimer's view, Russia and the West have been operating with totally different handbooks. Putin and his compatriots have been thinking and acting as realists, whereas Washington remains adhered to progressive liberal ideas about United States hegemony.

It is clear that the liberal hegemony of the past twenty-five years does not work. It has left a legacy of futile wars, failed diplomacy, and diminished prestige for the United States. The people who have paid the greatest cost for Washington's post-Cold War foreign policy are the foreigners who have had the misfortune of living in countries that American policy makers targeted for regime change.

---

5. Mearsheimer, 171.
6. Mearsheimer, 177.

Mearsheimer would prefer to remain on the theoretical or abstract level, addressing social engineering abroad and the failure of U.S. foreign policy in a general way, but he can't avoid illustrating what he is talking about. The United States, he charges, has been operating in countries its policy makers know little about. He finds that few government officials speak Arabic or even know the difference between Sunni and Shi'a Islam.

Perhaps the most egregious failure of the Obama administration, he maintains, was its attempt to bring down the legitimate government of Syria. Taking the side of a ragtag group rebelling against the government of Bashar al Assad, the United States demanded that Assad step down. Duly elected by his people, he refused. The United States then provided military and other support to "moderate" rebel groups. The CIA and the Pentagon spent more than $1.5 billion on weapons and the training of the dissidents. The strategy failed completely. Assad is still in power. More than 400,000 have died as a result of the U.S. intervention in the so-called "civil war." Almost half the population of Syria has been forced to flee their homes.

Another example of ill-conceived U.S. foreign policy is the State Department's meddling in the internal affairs of the government of the Ukraine. The trouble began when President Yanukovych rejected a major economic deal he had been negotiating with the European Union and decided instead to accept a counteroffer from Russia. That decision led to protests against the government in Kiev. The United States immediately backed the coup. Senator McCain and other U.S. officials participated in the Maidan Square demonstrations. A U.S. government official later publicly admitted that the United States spent $5 billion to bring about the removal of Yanukovych and provided support for the civil war that followed.

*The Great Delusion* does not end on a happy note. "The case for a realist based foreign policy is straight forward," writes John Mearsheimer, "and it should be compelling to a large majority of Americans. But it is still a tough sell, mainly because many in the foreign policy elite are deeply committed to liberal hegemony and will go to enormous lengths to defend it."[7]

---

7. Mearsheimer, 233.

# ~20~
# Physics and Philosophy

There can be no conflict between philosophy and the natural sciences any more than between theology and the natural sciences, as long as both remain true to their methods. Conflicts do arise between physicists and philosophers or biologists and theologians largely because of misunderstanding, sometimes aided and abetted by the propensity of some to publish in the *New York Times*. The sciences thus reported come laden with metaphor. We hear of "anti-matter," "drops of electricity," "black holes," "right- or left-handed spin of a K-meson," and I haven't even mentioned "string theory." In the early 1950s, when someone at the University of California introduced the concept of "anti-matter," one of my graduate student classmates, in trying to elucidate the term for a newspaper reporter, ended up being presented as refuting an eminent physicist at Berkeley. He was merely trying to unpack the metaphor. Burnt once, he accepted the advice of another classmate: "When you see a reporter, run, not walk, the other way." My classmate and lifelong friend survived some mild ridicule, and after earning his doctorate at The Catholic University of America, he eventually became chairman of the physics department at a major research university.

Of course, there is the well-known case of Galileo, who tried to teach biblical scholars how to interpret Scripture and whose work in return was subjected to scrutiny. As many know, he got caught teaching a likely hypothesis as if it were demonstrated fact. We all know that Darwin was supposed to have done away with a creative God, whether he said so or not. And Einstein removed moral constraint with his theory of relativity. It is likely that both Einstein and Heisenberg were amused by the misuse of terms associated with their names. Then there is the more recent episode of James Watson and Francis Crick, the discoverers of the double helix structure of DNA. Crick, reflecting on his landmark work in human genetics, asserted, "The God hypothesis is rather discredited." Watson similarly concluded, "Only with the discovery of the double helix and the ensuing genetic revolution have we had grounds for thinking that the power held traditionally to be the exclusive property of the gods might one day be ours."[1]

Journalists on both sides of the Atlantic are only too willing to seize upon an ambiguous metaphor to undermine Christian belief in a benevolent God or to discard biblical standards of morality. And we have come to expect that of them. But when physicists and other natural scientists transfer their authority from their legitimate domain to areas that are philosophical and theological, their motives become suspect.

Of course, the physicist, chemist, or biologist is a product of his early education, wherein he has likely incurred a critique of the Western intellectual tradition in the Enlightenment manner. John Dewey's educational philosophy that has long prevailed in academic circles can be summed up in one sentence: The function of education is not to transmit an inherited intellectual tradition but to subject it to criticism. When it came to morality, Dewey was cautious. Biblical morality was not to be rejected outright, but a proper or secular

---

1. James Watson and Francis Crick, quoted in "DNA Pioneers Lash Out at Religion," *The Washington Times*, March 24, 2003, https://www.washingtontimes.com/news/2003/mar/24/20030324-090202-5705r/.

rationale was to be sought for those values retained after a sifting takes place.

The necessity of providing the modern mind with an adequate interpretation of natural science is a task inherited from the eighteenth century, wherein Locke and Hume challenged the notions of "substance" and "causality" and thereby undermined a classical understanding of science. The awakened Kant accepted Hume's psychological account of causality and went on to develop a theory of knowledge that had repercussions in the philosophical world and beyond. The emphasis Kant placed on the categories as mental structures whose function consisted mainly in organizing data received by the senses had a profound effect on the common understanding of science. Karl Popper, in questioning the value of induction, may be regarded as pursuing empiricism to its logical consequence.

Ancient notions of science presupposed through the Renaissance, certainly by Copernicus, Galileo, and Kepler, as well as their contemporaries, assumed the intelligibility of nature and the power of mind to ferret out the secrets of nature. With roots in Plato, Aristotle, and the Scholastics, philosophical realism was the coin of the day, but with the advent of British empiricism, the common understanding of the nature of science was transformed. When Kant asked how science is possible whereas metaphysics is not, his answer was no help. Having acquiesced to Locke and Hume he was led, not to skepticism, but to a peculiar kind of faith wherein the assumption of postulates provided the foundation of both physics and belief in God. Old ideas—God, nature, soul—were not to be dismissed but to be reinterpreted and retained merely for their regulative value.

The positivism spawned by eighteenth century empiricism in effect reduced knowledge to sensory experience. Given its premises, we can only believe what we sensorially encounter.

On the basis of what we observe we can make predictions—assuming the accuracy of our description and the adequacy of our mathematics—about what may happen in the future. What things are in themselves, *noumena*, remain unknown. On this account, description replaces definition in the Aristotelian sense. Some theorists have gone so far as to say that all we know is the reaction of natural phenomena to our instruments—in extreme cases the readings on a dial. For someone such as Carl Hempel or Ernest Nagel an explanation becomes a hypothesis to be tested for adequacy. A hypothesis is a conceptual scheme that not only enables data to be correlated but signals certain results when the integration of its components is established.

An amusing account may illustrate the point being made here. Wolfgang Pauli in 1930 postulated the existence of an undetected particle to account for phenomena he could not otherwise explain. Perhaps tongue in cheek, he apologized in the atmosphere of the academic Zeitgeist, reportedly saying, "I have done a terrible thing today.... I have suggested something that can never be verified experimentally."[2] Supporting Pauli, the Italian physicist Enrico Fermi baptized the hypothetical particle "neutrino," or "little neutral one," but his paper was rejected by the prestigious journal *Nature* as too speculative and remote from reality. The first experiment to hunt for the neutrino was called "Project Poltergeist." In 1956 Clyde Cowan and Fred Reines found a definite trace of the elusive neutrino as a result of experiments performed with a newly commissioned reactor at Los Alamos. Pauli, in an Aristotelian manner, was seeking an explanation, reasoning from effect to unseen cause—but clearly, he was out of line as judged by positivistic canons.

2. Fred Hoyle, "Concluding Remarks," *Proceedings of the Royal Society of London*, Series A 301 (1967): 171.

It is my contention that the eighteenth century British empiricism as found in Locke and Hume is incompatible with contemporary science. From an Aristotelian point of view the object of scientific inquiry is the essence or nature of material things as inferred from their behavior. Things are what their nature's activity discloses them to be. Nature is understood as the whatness or quiddity of a thing, the source of its activity, both active and passive, a synonym for essence considered dynamically.

The empiricist is right when he affirms that essence or nature is not given sensorially, that is, in the sense report. But there is more in the sense report than the senses themselves are able to appreciate. The sense report of a common element is a report of its accidental features, such as color, resistance to pressure, relative weight, and perhaps odor. Locke declared that what we call a "substance" is nothing more than the name we give to our mental collation of these properties. The substance itself remains an unknown substrate. In this one hears echoes of Ockham!

Couple Locke's account of substance with Hume's account of causality and you have the repudiation of science in the Aristotelian sense. For Aristotle the aim of scientific inquiry is to explain something that is unintelligible taken by itself. To have scientific knowledge is to know why things are the way they are or behave the way they do. The basis of explanation is the principle of sufficient reason. To know the *propter quid* is a mark of success, the end of a quest. Given the complexity of nature, the quest is apt to be open-ended in the sense that there is always more to know. A provisional explanation may give way to a fuller one without the repudiation of a previous one. Thus, a pre-scientific knowledge of materials or processes can lead to a scientific one. The ancients well knew the properties of copper, its malleability, its relative softness, and in a vague way its melting point and its ability to form compounds with other metals. The molecular structure responsible for these properties, of course, eluded them.

To continue this discussion, it is necessary to focus on two related notions that play an important role in an Aristotelian account of science. The first is the notion of potentiality; the second, the concept of nature or, in contemporary epistemology, its more or less equivalent: structure and our mental representation of such by means of models. From an Aristotelian point of view, contemporary attempts to model are attempts to grasp by means of equations or visual aids the structure responsible for behavior, the locus of potentiality. Aristotle was convinced that there is no intellection without accompanying sensation; today we use the term "model."

It is the Aristotelian notion of "potentiality" and its related notions of capacity, power, and possibility that come into play. Under the influence of Gilbert Ryle (1900–1976), statements about disposition have come to be treated as hypothetical or conditional statements or as conjunctions of such statements.[3] "He is intelligent" is taken to mean that if he is presented with a problem, he will quickly produce a solution. It is easy to transform a declarative sentence about what is into a modal assertion about what may be expected. "The vase is fragile" becomes, "If dropped, it will break." Avoided is the ascription of an inherent property or the recognition of a real capacity. The commonsense recognition that capacities imply a subject, the ontological grounding of possibility, is put aside.

---

3. Gilbert Ryle, *The Concept of Mind*, first published 1949; numerous editions. See the edition that contains a valuable introduction by Daniel C. Dennett (Chicago: University of Chicago Press, 2002).

The ability to deal with the concept of potentiality is a major test for any philosophy of science. How the issue is treated divides not only idealist from realist but also metaphysician from logician. There is ample evidence that those who write about possible worlds tend to blur, if not confuse, logical and material possibility. Logicians by trade are inclined to pay no attention to the way premises are obtained. Logic deals with judgments as it finds them; its subject matter is given. Since logical and mathematical truths are universal and necessary, it is tempting to think of them as eternal and to relate them to the actual as if the relation were that of the determinable to the determinate. The logician is tempted to speak of existence as a determination that happens to a possible essence. Thus, conceptually, whatever is possible may be instantiated.

The careful logician will, of course, avoid the trap. He is aware that the manifold of merely possible things is an intellectual construct, and that the starting point of this construct is an informed view of the real world as provided by the sciences. In common with the realist, he recognizes that intellectual construction is subject to the implicit constraint of the given that one must acknowledge the distinction between real or physical possibility and the strictly hypothetical. The physically possible is governed by the laws of nature. Even from a logical point of view, the really possible is that which is consistent with a certain body of stipulated fact. But how to determine that consistency? Is all that is not intrinsically self-contradictory possible? As long as we remain in the order of abstract possibility, whatever is not blatantly self-contradictory can be said to be possible. But as soon as we enter the order of existence, impossibilities begin to multiply. If existence is imparted to any one structure, some others become impossible.

This can be illustrated by the difference between the artist and the art critic. Artists, painters, sculptors, and musicians always function in an existential situation. Either the form is found in marble, as Michelangelo proclaimed, or is dictated by material contingencies. The critic, not so constrained, is free to imagine possibilities contrary to the structures available to the artist. Who has not experienced the critic who, in the light of ideals inappropriate or impossible to attain, nevertheless finds fault with the artifact before him. Something like this occurs in the political order, where the ideal frequently drives out the good.

From a realist perspective, if we talk about possibilities, we do not ordinarily concern ourselves with logical possibility. Logical and mathematical truths are universal and necessary possibilities, and about them we do not deliberate. Nor do we normally deliberate about the content of a creative imagination at play. Such imagination feeds on intelligible factors drawn from experience.

From the realist perspective, it is capacity, tendency, and disposition on the part of physical objects that are at once the ground of logical possibility, artistic imagination, and the object of scientific inquiry. In determining what is materially possible, reference—of necessity—is made to empirical laws, that is, to laws of nature or to statistical evidence pertaining to what has been observed to be the case. The potentialities recognized in things are permanent features of those things. They are predicated of those things whether or not they are acting or being stimulated. We utilize copper tubing because of its resistance to corrosion and because of its ability to conduct heat effectively, and similarly we use copper wire because it is capable of conducting electricity. We mark FRAGILE on packages because we know something about the glass structure and its inherent properties. The capacity to break does not consist in the occurrence of the event. It seems forced to construe fragility in modal terms such that we say or imply something like: A fragile piece of glass is one that would break in some possible world in which, unlike the present world, it is actually being dropped.

The reason we believe that a certain disposition can be asserted of a subject is that we know that it currently has such and such power. Thus, to ascribe a power to a thing or material is to say something about what it can or will do. To merely specify external conditions is not enough. Circumstances may change without affecting the thing itself. To ascribe a power is to ascribe a disposition to a specific subject because we have some insight into the nature or structure of the thing.

The term "magnetic" is another example of a disposition term. It designates not a directly observable characteristic but rather a disposition on the part of some physical object to display a specific reaction under certain circumstances. The vocabulary of natural science abounds in dispositional terms such as "malleable," "elastic," "conductor" of heat, "fissionable," "recessive trait," and the like. Are these features not as real as any empirically discernable property we may predicate? Does not structure as disclosed through previous behavior manifest real disposition? Unavoidable is the inclination to form some sort of a conceptual aid as we attempt to understand the mechanism responsible for the activity under consideration. Those who favor a contextual approach merely describe, not explain. The subjunctive conditional, while not inaccurate, nevertheless flies in the face of the way we normally think and speak about things. Only by recognizing a physical connection between the nature of a thing and the way it acts do we find the root of conceptual connections employed in talk of material and logical possibility.

We need not suppose that every capacity or disposition of magnesium that we have identified requires the attribution of a power. There is reason to argue that diverse dispositions may be manifestations of the same power. In fact, dispositions attributed to a thing may be nothing more than structure viewed from several vantage points. On the other hand, as we move from atom to molecule, to compound, to organism, powers are more easily discerned, particularly when the subject is animate. Since antiquity, cognitive and appetitive powers have been distinguished, and both distinguished from the purely vegetative. The list has never been very long, and always where encountered, identification is thought to follow empirically ascertained evidence. An old Scholastic maxim is that powers are specified by behavior, behavior by object. Unless demanded by the evidence, nothing is inferred, nothing is predicated of a subject. The processes of attribution and, negatively, of elimination are by no means simple. The lower the order, the more constant or invariable the nature. The more sophisticated our knowledge of things becomes, the more we understand their mechanism to confer and receive. In dealing with relatively simple structures at the atomic or molecular level, the identification of the molecular structure may be simply the identification of the power. Molecular structure may itself be the only capacity we need to recognize in order to account for an element's physical or chemical behavior. Structure itself is, after all, a disposition of parts. The more we know about those parts and their relation to each other, the more we can determine (predict) what is possible. To say this is not to subscribe to a mechanistic interpretation but to recognize that powers are closely related to natures that manifest them. J. L. Mackie would banish altogether the notion of power and settle for a purely descriptive account.[4] The

---

4. John Leslie Mackie, *Cement of the Universe: A Study of Causation* (Oxford: Clarendon Press, 1974).

metaphysician, he thinks, is affected with double vision. But to the realist, the distinctions between thing and disposition, between disposition and activity, are real and when acknowledged assist in rendering intelligible the phenomena that require explanation.

As Rom Harré has argued, scientific knowledge consists primarily in a knowledge of the internal structures of persisting things and materials; secondarily, in the knowledge of the statistics of events, of the behavior of such things and materials, wherein one discerns patterns among these events through certain types of change and not through other kinds. Emphasis is placed on structures and their persistence.[5] The recognition of such units and their differentiation is the recognition of natural kinds. The chemical analysis of a material, the genes inherited from a parent, the structure of a crystal, the electronic configuration of an atom, all point to real natures or essences. In them reside the powers of generation and production; it is through their operation that the flux of events results. On this account, a scientific explanation consists principally in accounting for the second type of information in terms of the first. A scientific explanation shows how the patterns discerned amidst the flux of events are produced by the persisting natures and constitutions of things.

There are many ways in which we mentally capture and communicate our knowledge of the structures under consideration. We use sentences to represent and communicate linguistically, but linguistic vehicles are not the only vehicles of thought. Pictures, models, and diagrams are also vehicles of thought. To draw a diagram or to make a model is to think. To

5. Rom Harré, *The Principles of Scientific Thinking*, ch. 4, "Laws of Nature" (Chicago: University of Chicago Press, 1970), 92–126.

construct a diagram, a picture, or a model is to attempt to get at the inner structure or constitution of a thing. The twentieth century preoccupation with linguistic vehicles such as declarative sentences and hypothetical propositions has blinded us to the structural picture from which they have been abstracted. Conditional statements are more apt to call attention to the possibilities of change, to the successive states of things, than to the structure of the things themselves. The two approaches, needless to say, are complementary; structure may be presented diagrammatically by means of pictures and models; the possibilities of change may be presented sententiously as conditional statements.

Pictures, models, and diagrams are metaphors or forms of analogy not unlike those we employ in ordinary discourse. In scientific as well as in ordinary speech, analogy functions to make available the less known in terms of the better known. Natural science is so permeated with metaphor that its use goes almost unnoticed. Lord Kelvin once said that he could not understand anything except insofar as he could construct a model. In physics, we speak of light waves, talk about heat as fluid, gases as if they consisted of plastic particles, electricity as a current, drops of electricity, anti-matter, right-handed and left-handed spin on a K meson; we talk of Faraday's strained space, electron quantum jumps, and star creation. In spite of the widespread employment of metaphor in the sciences, one encounters few theories of their function.

Parenthetically it may be noted that theories of analogy first came into being in an attempt to understand how metaphysics could speak of things divine and not slip into either agnosticism or anthropomorphism. This is not to suggest that common metaphors in the sciences function in exactly the same way as they do in theological discourse. In ordinary prescientific knowledge, just as in scientific knowledge, metaphor plays a heuristic role, revealing semi-disclosed aspects of things and suggesting new ways to look at things. Or perhaps I should put it the other way around. The scientific employment of metaphors, analogies, and models is not unlike their use in everyday coming-to-know. The value of a prescientific knowledge of things tends to be under-acknowledged. Overlooked is the continuity between the two types of prescientific and scientific knowledge. Things and processes that form the object of scientific knowledge are known in a vague or imprecise manner before they become objects of the controlled and systematic knowledge, which is science. One of the unfortunate effects of certain nineteenth century theories of science was to place the emphasis upon mathematics and experiment divorced from our personal contributions in using them, thus creating a gulf between science and life.

Natural scientists in much of their theoretical activity are, in fact, trying to form a mental picture of the mechanisms of nature that are responsible for the phenomena they observe. The forming of a mental picture, in effect, is the making of models. Models may be sentential or iconic. A model may be nothing more than a tentative analogue for the real but as yet unknown mechanism or structure. The model itself may be fashioned on things we know or understand only imperfectly. When theory construction is successful, that which is presented as a model of an unknown mechanism in one generation may in another generation be seen to approximate the physical structure of the object in question. In the lifetime of our fathers, if not in our own lifetime, the molecular structure of a solid was a mere postulate, a crude analogue to represent what was thought ought to be the case on the basis of the evidence at hand. Today an electron microscope can take directly interpretable pictures of atoms within solids. Now we can understand why some solids behave as insulators, others as semiconductors, and still others as metals. To use another example, with nuclear magnetic resonance imaging we are able to determine sodium or phosphorus concentrations in compounds such as fats and carbohydrates in the living tissues of the human body. Various nineteenth century models of the cell and its components in the twentieth century turned out to be a close approximation of the postulated structure.

Models approximate structure when adequate. We had a visual model of the cell long before we saw it with a microscope. The double-helix structure responsible for the inheritance of genetic traits was an iconic model long before the electron microscope confirmed it. The inference to many chemical and subatomic structures has been supported in a plurality of ways as our instruments have become more sophisticated. As our knowledge of the structures of things becomes more refined, we can understand why things behave as they do. But no matter how revealing structure may be, it is not metaphysically ultimate from an Aristotelian point of view. For Aristotle, structure is a proper accident, the manifestation of a composite essence, an essence composed of matter and form. The many distinctions he introduces in his attempt to account for becoming not only give him a theory of reality but contribute to his theory of knowledge.

A final thought: from an Aristotelian perspective, models, pictures, and diagrams are created in an attempt to understand the natures of things. In some instances, they may be little more than visual aids, but more often than not they express insights into natures that exist independently of the mind. Since the accumulation of knowledge is an ongoing process, no model is ever likely to be complete. The ontological richness of even the simplest structure is apt to require revision after revision. We can never plumb the depths of the beings that we encounter. If biography after biography is sometimes required to fathom the personality of a great man, so too the science accumulated over century after century may be required to intellectually approximate nature's structures. Model supplants model, each incorporating preceding discoveries. It is rare that the false is supplanted with the true; rather the less adequate account is usually enriched or replaced by the more adequate.

## ~21~
# C. S. Peirce, Jacques Maritain, and Other Scholastics on the Problem of Induction

THE NECESSITY OF PROVIDING an adequate interpretation of natural science is a task inherited from the eighteenth century, wherein John Locke and David Hume challenged the Aristotelian notions of substance and causality and thereby undermined a classical understanding of science. The awakened Kant accepted Hume's psychological account of causality and went on to ask: how is science possible whereas metaphysics is not? Peirce escaped both the empiricist trap and the fideism that followed Kant's *Critique*.

Charles Sanders Peirce has to be regarded as one of the foremost American philosophers of the late eighteenth and early nineteenth centuries, one of a small band of great knowers that included William James, Josiah Royce, and George Santayana. A logician and philosopher of science, Peirce is best known for his work on the logic of relations and his promotion of pragmatism as a method of research. He never wrote a book, but his collected papers, edited and published posthumously by the *Peirce Edition of Indiana University*, run to eight volumes.

In his discussion of the nature of science, Peirce introduces the notion of "abduction" as distinct from induction. Abduction is the process of forming an explanatory hypothesis. The process starts with observation and then seeks to find the simplest and most likely explanation for the phenomena encountered, but unlike inductive reasoning, its premises do not guarantee any conclusion. One can understand abductive reasoning as inference only to the best explanation available. It falls short of demonstration.

In accord with his general outlook, Peirce regards belief in God as reasonable. "There are no significant, strong, countervailing reasons to disbelief in God's reality. The more one ponders the reality of God, the more he will respond in every part of his mind to its beauty, for its supplying an ideal of life and for its thoroughly satisfactory explanation of the whole environment." Peirce develops these insights in his 1892 article, "A Neglected Argument for the Reality of God." Elsewhere in this article he says, "God . . . is *the* definable proper name, signifying *ens necessarium*."[1] And "We must not predicate any attribute of God otherwise than vaguely and figuratively, since God, though in a sense essentially intelligible, is nevertheless essentially incomprehensible."[2] From abduction, Peirce has moved to deduction.

Maritain himself offers one of the best expositions and defense of the perennial value of the Aristotelian account of induction. His account is developed sequentially in three works, which may be read in tandem. I have in mind Maritain's *Introduction to Philosophy* (1917), his *Formal Logic* (1937), and his *Degrees of Knowledge* (1959). Although Jacques Maritain is the focus of this presentation, this is not to ignore the

1. Charles Sanders Peirce, "A Neglected Argument for the Reality of God," *Hibbert Journal* 7, no. 90 (1908).

2. Peirce, "Significs and Logic," (Nov. 3–18, 1909) in *The Charles Peirce Papers*, as identified by Richard Robin, Houghton Library of Harvard University, no. 641: 22, cited in Richard Kenneth Atkins, *Peirce and the Conduct of Life: Sentiment and Instincts in Ethics and Religion* (Cambridge: Cambridge University Press, 2016), 85.

similar work of Louis Groarke, *An Aristotelian Account of Induction* (2009); Stephen Gaukroger, *The Emergence of a Scientific Culture* (2006); and Allan Bach, *Aristotle's Theory of Abstraction* (2014).

Maritain distinguishes between what the Scholastics call the proper object of the senses (color, shape, magnitude, and odor) and that of the intellect (a spontaneous insight into the nature or essence of a thing under consideration). Maritain has his own way of expressing this insight. He writes: "Induction [by incomplete enumeration] does not make us pass from some to ALL . . . but from some to EVERY." We should avoid saying "all metals conduct electricity" and instead, say "metal conducts electricity." It is the intellect's grasp of "the universal nature" of metal that enables it to attribute the "same predicate to each" individual metal.[3]

Induction, holds Maritain, has the double function of inference and proof. Induction admits of a certain zone of probability. It is, in fact, neither an inference properly so-called, nor an argument; it merely leads the mind to a connection of terms, whose intelligible necessity is perceived immediately. Peirce has said as much.

In this context Maritain calls attention to a distinction between what belongs to logic itself and what belongs to epistemology or metaphysics. It belongs to metaphysics to discuss nominalism and realism and the controversies concerning the nature of science and ordinary knowledge. The discussion of the first principles of thought and being and the order in which they are known to us is also a part of metaphysics.

Louis Groarke, in his *Aristotelian Account of Induction*, develops Maritain's thesis, offering yet another telling critique

---

3. Jacques Maritain, *Formal Logic*, trans. Imelda Choquette (New York: Sheed & Ward, 1937), 271.

of both the empiricist's account of induction and the empiricist's notion of substance. Like Étienne Gilson and Maritain, upon whom he draws, Groarke is conscious of the historical setting of philosophical analysis and debate. He is convinced that no historical idea arrives at the scene without some kind of antecedent. Descartes may have set out to create a new philosophy—both natural and philosophical—to take the place of Aristotle and Aquinas, yet the historian Jorge Secada, in his careful study of Descartes, finds it necessary to give his book the subtitle: *The Scholastic Origins of Modern Philosophy*.

Groarke reminds his reader, "Scientific induction is, for Aristotle, a matter of understanding what must be the case; it is the capacity of insight (not argument) that allows us to make logical sense of observation."[4] Confronted with repeated instances of phenomena, human reason arrives at a universal principle: water runs downhill, copper conducts electricity, alcohol is intoxicating. Induction is the mental ability to jump from the experience of the particular to concepts, rules and principles covering a wide variety of cases. We can look upon induction in two ways, says Groarke. Induction as traditionally understood is an inference from the particular to the universal, but it is also an inference from sense perception to the intelligible.

After Francis Bacon, the praise of induction was taken to be a sign of enlightenment. Today popular science writers repeat the all too familiar tale about the triumph of modern science over natural philosophy, and the public largely accepts the story because it lacks historical knowledge and the philosophical sophistication necessary to free itself from the reigning ortho-

---

4. Louis Groarke, *An Aristotelian Account of Induction: Creating Something from Nothing* (Montreal: McGill-Queen's University, 2009), 27.

doxy. In fact, those that did the most to advance the sciences and the nature of scientific explanation did not refute or even repudiate ancient notions concerning the object of science and the nature of scientific explanation: they merely shifted discourse from considerations of nature or essence of things to that which can be measured, but in doing so they neglected to integrate the scientific tableau of the new physics with that of philosophy and common sense.

Rémi Brague, who many know as the author of *The Legend of the Middle Ages* and *Eccentric Culture*, is not only a historian but a philosopher of note.[5] In the spirit of Maritain, Brague, in his Medalist Address to the American Catholic Philosophical Association in 2015, issued a pertinent call. "We badly need a philosophy of nature," he said. "First; there is the Natural Philosophy such as it is still taught in Cambridge from the chair once occupied by Isaac Newton, i.e., physics as a description of natural things, together with the writing of their laws in rigorous mathematical language.

"Second, there is the inquiry into the basic concepts of natural science; to begin with, nature, motion, time, space, or whatnot. This was the main subject matter of Aristotle's *Physics*."[6]

In Brague's judgment, ancient philosophy provided a rudimentary description of nature and furnished us with an understanding of nature. Heavy bodies fall and light bodies go upward because they strive to reach their natural abodes where they find their specific fulfillment, their good. Modern physics has

5. See chapter 15 of this volume.
6. Brague, "On the Need for a Philosophy of Nature and on Aquinas's Help in Sketching One," *Proceedings of the American Catholic Philosophical Association* 89 (2015): 35.

gotten rid of that explanation. We are faced now with an explanation that we cannot accept any longer and a description that doesn't allow us to really understand anything. Understanding, he insists, requires an acknowledgment of purpose in nature. In the final analysis we cannot avoid talking about creation.

Brague continues, "We can write the laws of the physical universe in the precise and rigorous language of mathematics, but we don't *understand* it in the strict meaning of 'understanding.' Nature can be described in a very accurate way, and we can on the basis of this description perform many technical wonders."[7] But this comes at the expense of a clear understanding of nature. From the physicist's point of view, reference to final causes "can be tolerated in the study of living organisms, for want of anything better, as long as we have not found the mechanism that accounts for what we want to explain."[8] We are assured by neurobiologists that a purely materialistic explanation is forthcoming.

There is no obvious point at which Newtonian physics replaced the old order of Aristotelian natural philosophy any more than there is an obvious point at which the Newtonian order gave way to the new order of quantum physics. For the contemporary physicist, it does not matter that the symbols and mathematics used to describe the quantum world defy the imagination, for it is not necessary to visualize the quantum world. So long as the physicist's calculations match his experimental results, it does not matter that the symbols and mathematics have any link to the physical world.

Nobel laureate Murray Gell-Mann is attributed as saying of quantam theory, "We all know how to use it and apply it to prob-

7. Brague, 37.
8. Brague, 37.

lems, and so we have learned to live with the fact that nobody can understand it."⁹ After approximately ninety years, physicists still have trouble reconciling the Newtonian and quantum worlds. And I haven't even mentioned string theory. The late Gian Carlo Rota, a professor of mathematics at MIT and student of Husserl, in dinner table conversation, with reference to contemporary theoretical physics, said "There is nothing for you philosophers to be disturbed about, i.e., accounts of the latest theoretical postulates as reported in the *New York Times*: Big Bang, black holes, dark matter, dark energy, Bohmian trajectories, collapsing stars, those postulates are nothing but a set of equations."

It comes down to this. A mathematical reading of the sensible world cannot speak the last word about the physical real. Physico-mathematical knowledge does not exhaust all that can be known about the physical real. We cannot ask such an account to give an ontological explanation of the sensible real, let alone account for human thought and volition. Tempting though it may be, a mechanistic philosophy that endeavors to explain everything in terms of extension and movement neglects an understanding of the spiritual dimension of man, although some remain confident that some version of the genome project will eventually shed light on the biological source of moral disposition and of morality itself.[10] I will return to this in a moment.

---

9. Widely reported without giving when or where it was written or said. For instance, see L. Wolpert, *The Unnatural Nature of Science* (Cambridge, Mass.: Harvard University Press, 1993), 144.

10. The Human Genome Project originated in 1990 and was initially headed by James D. Watson at the U.S. National Institutes of Health. Its purpose was to understand and to map the genetic makeup of the human species.

I would be remiss if I did not say something about Edith Stein and her solution to the problem of individuation. Stein may not have been a regular attendee at Maritain's intellectual soirées in Paris, but we know that she did attend some sessions, perhaps in the company of Ernest Psichari, who had introduced her to St. Thomas. As a matter of fact, it was Psichari who introduced Maritain to St. Thomas. Léon Bloy may have been instrumental with respect to Maritain's conversion to Catholicism, but it was Psichari who gave him his intellectual compass, even though Maritain has said that he was a Thomist before he read a word of St. Thomas.

As a personalist, Edith Stein approached the topic from the reverse problem of accounting for the individual, given the universal. In her *habilitationsschrift*, written under the direction of Edmund Husserl and published posthumously as *Finite and Eternal Being*, she tackles the problem of individuation while acknowledging a common human nature. A person is not simply an exemplification of a common human nature. A person is not like all others with the common human form. A person has a level of unrepeatability and dignity that the classic Aristotelian position does not address.

This leads Stein to an extended discussion of the principle of individuation. Her position may be described as uniquely her own—neither that of Aquinas nor that of Duns Scotus. She speaks of "a common human form" where Aquinas would speak of a common human nature. Although influenced by St. Thomas

---

It was thought of as necessary to ensure the continuing progress of medicine and other health sciences. The project was designed to identify the approximate 2,400 genes in the human person, but eventually the authors found it necessary to address some of the ethical, legal, and social issues that arose from the availability of genetic information.

in much of her work, she has a distinctive metaphysical conception of being and essence. She wants to give an account of how there can be many instances of the same types that differ numerically but also qualitatively. She does this by positing a form in addition to the common human form—not exactly Scotus's formal principle of individuation (the principle of *haecceitas*), but closer to Scotus than Aquinas's *signate matter*. Stein is concerned not so much with individuation as she is with uniqueness.[11] To fully understand her position, one would have to invoke Husserl's theory of parts and wholes as presented in his *Logical Investigations III*.

Maritain, Peirce, and Brague, it should be noted, write from an Aristotelian point of view. From their or any other perspective, it is difficult to write about science in the abstract. There are many sciences, each employing a methodology of its own appropriate to its object of study. The Latin term, *scientia*, means knowledge, but not all knowledge can claim to be scientific. Enumeration is not science, nor is technology to be equated with science, though it is often thought of as science. Precise observation is not science, nor is a correlation of data that at first blush seems to be related. We speak of medical science when we mean the art of medicine. Engineering, too, is thought of as science—but, like medicine, engineering draws upon a wealth of scientifically derived information but is not itself a science. The application of scientifically derived information is essentially an art with its own rules of application, much like prudence is the application of wisdom. We may not think of theology as a science, but Aristotle made room for

---

11. See Sarah Borden Sharkey, *Thine Own Self: Individuality in Edith Stein's Later Writings* (Washington, D.C.: The Catholic University of America Press, 2010), 210.

"divine science." Today we call it natural theology and distinguish it from sacred theology—that is, from theology that has as its premises propositions derived from revelation. There is a whole cadre of disciplines we categorize as social science, but most of the time when we talk about science, we have in mind natural science.

A philosophy of science is but part of one's overarching metaphysics, but even so, most accounts are partly shaped by the intellectual milieu in which they arise. Traditional metaphysical issues, including substance, causality, and purpose, all have a bearing on how science is understood. Where these realties are denied, skepticism and materialism are likely to prevail. Science is then reduced to description and prediction, with implications beyond the confines of the academy, especially on the direction that American education was to take at all levels. If there is no evidence for the existence of God or order in nature, the student will miss the spiritual and moral component of life. Any visible reference to the Hebrew Decalogue is likely to have been removed from his school.

Here a historical footnote may be in order. In the early days of the American republic, philosophy was the province of New England divines, those same ministers who laid the foundations of what were to become some of America's most prestigious universities. By the end of the eighteenth century, it was recognized that British empiricism and Enlightenment philosophy, originating in France and Germany, were posing a threat to Christian faith. The *Journal of Speculative Philosophy*, the first journal of philosophy in the English language, was founded at St. Louis in 1867, among other reasons, to combat the secular philosophies arriving from Europe. The chosen mode of counterattack was that of German idealism, particularly the idealism of Hegel. In its first issue its editor, William Torrey Harris, explained the purpose of the journal. He gave three reasons. In his judgment, speculative philosophy provides, first, a philosophy of religion much needed at a time when traditional religious teaching and ecclesial authority were losing their influence. Second, it provides a social philosophy compatible with a communal outlook, as contrasted to a devastating individualism. Third, while taking cognizance of the startling advances in the natural sciences, it provides an alternative to empiricism as a philosophy of knowledge. Speculative philosophy for Harris is a tradition that begins with Plato, a tradition that finds its full expression in Hegel.

The foremost representative of the speculative philosophy endorsed by Harris was undoubtedly Josiah Royce, whose Gifford lectures (1900–1901), published as *The World and the Individual*, sought not only to counter the skepticism of the day, but to provide a rational foundation for the Christian faith. Royce had little respect for blind faith, a response created by Kant's destruction of metaphysics. In 1888, Royce wrote, "We all live, philosophically speaking, in a Kantian atmosphere."[12] Eschewing the outright voluntarism of Schopenhauer, Royce sought a metaphysics that would rationally permit him to embrace his Christian heritage.

Whereas William James was convinced that every demonstrative approach to God must fail, Royce was convinced that speculative reason gives one access to God. The code words of the day—evolution, progress, illusion, higher criticism, communism, socialism—he thought evoked a mental outlook that reduced Christianity to metaphor and Christian organizations to welfare dispensaries. What was at issue for Royce was not

12. Josiah Royce, "Before and since Kant," *The Berkely Quarterly* 2 (January 1881): 134.

simply a philosophical problem; the philosophers also tutored the architects of the new biblical criticism, the *Redaktionsgeschichte* movement.

David Fredrich Strauss, in his *Das Leben Jesu*, under the influence of the Enlightenment, examined the Gospels and the life of Jesus from the standpoint of higher criticism and concluded that Christ was not God but a supremely good man whose moral imperatives deserved to be followed. This Royce could not accept; there is no philosophically compelling reason, he maintained, to embrace a purely naturalistic interpretation of the sacred scriptures. The movement inspired by Royce was not without success. By the last quarter of the nineteenth century, nearly every chair of philosophy in the emerging universities was held by an idealist.

But the intellectual climate was soon to change. Hegel was not able to hold the day in the face of notable achievements in the sciences that demanded recognition of the empirical source of new ways of thinking about nature. Laws of nature are discovered: inquiry is not simply the uncovering of the implicit or the organization of data in the light of the given. To Royce's supposed definitive critique of materialism, opposition was not long in coming. Critiques were mounted in volumes published as corporate philosophical inquiry, under titles such as *The New Realism* (1912) and *Critical Realism* (1920) and were soon to control the day. By 1916, the idealism of the Saint Louis Hegelians, as they had come to be called, had given way and would soon be replaced by the pragmatic naturalism of John Dewey and his school. Dewey's outlook found expression in another corporate volume, *Naturalism and the Human Spirit* (1944). This signaled the direction the new realism was to take. Under the influence of W. H. Kirkpatrick and Dewey, it became the philosophy undergirding public education in the United States.

To come to a conclusion: the solution to a seemingly irrelevant philosophical problem has much to do with how we live. Are we the occupants of a purely materialistic world as the empiricist would have it, or are we the beneficiaries of an ordered universe, designed by a creator who gave us an intellect able to grasp the immaterial as well as the material aspects of our world? You know my answer. As Alice objected to the view of the Red King in Lewis Carroll's *Through the Looking-Glass*, "I don't like belonging to another person's dream."[13]

---

13. Lewis Carroll, *Alice's Adventures in Wonderland and Through the Looking-Glass* (New York: Bantam Dell, 1981), 196.

# Part IV

## ❧22❧
# Christopher Dawson and the Survival of Western Culture

"DURING THE LAST TWO CENTURIES, the human race has experienced the greatest changes that it has known since the beginnings of recorded history."[1] So wrote Christopher Dawson, the distinguished British historian, in 1948. This transformation, he tells the reader, had its source in a particular society in a particular civilization, that is, Europe. The change was "at once a political revolution, an economic revolution and a scientific evolution." But that is not all, as Dawson was able to show. "In order to understand European history we must first understand," wrote Dawson, "what Europe is—not a mere geographical expression, nor a heterogeneous collection of independent nationalities, but a true society of peoples possessing a common tradition of culture and religion. In the past this social organism was known as Christendom."[2]

Dawson was not the first to notice the transformation. Frederick Nietzsche (1844–1900), an atheist and no friend of Christianity, as early as the nineteenth century observed, in his words, "The whole of the West no longer possess the instincts out of which institutions grow, out of which a *future* grows."[3] By

---
1. Christopher Dawson, *The Gods of the Revolution* (Washington, D.C.: The Catholic University of America Press, 2015), 1.
2. Dawson, 4.
3. Nietzsche, *Twilight of the Idols*, in *The Portable Nietzche*, ed. and trans. Walter Kaufmann (New York: Penguin Press, 1954), 543.

his time views entertained in the eighteenth and nineteenth century drawing rooms, and in the academy of those days, had made their way into the marketplace. The spirit of the time was both reflected and promoted by Denis Diderot (1713–1784), who produced a highly influential work known as the *Encyclopédie*. In the preface to the *Encyclopédie* he wrote, "Everything must be examined, everything must be shaken up, without exception and without circumspection."[4] Voltaire, Rousseau, and d'Alembert were prominent contributors to the *Encyclopédie*. Voltaire, like Rousseau, urged the eradication of Christianity from the world of higher culture, but he was willing to have it remain in the stables and in the scullery as a moral force, lest a servant class emancipated from traditional moral norms might pilfer.

Dawson finds: "The origins of modern Democracy are so closely bound up with the history of liberalism that it is a matter of considerable difficulty to disentangle them and to distinguish their distinctive contributions to the common political-tradition of modern western culture."[5] The English, French, and American Revolutions were liberal revolutions, Dawson maintains, the logical expressions of the philosophy promoted by the French philosophers and the impact of the French Revolution continues to this day.

On the Continent of Europe, the revolution of ideas preceded the political and social revolutions by a half century. The revolution of ideas was the work of a small minority, men of letters who looked to the princes and nobles of Europe rather than to the common people. The Church still maintained its

---

4. Quoted in Peter Gay, *The Enlightenment: An Interpretation*. Vol. 1, *The Rise of Modern Paganism* (New York: Publisher, 1966, repr.), 142.

5. Dawson, *The Gods of the Revolution*, 29.

influence over men's minds and its festivals and pilgrimages played a great part in the life of the people. There remained deep currents of religious life even in the century that followed.

The historic origins of liberalism take us back to Rousseau and the empiricism of the eighteenth century, which transformed our understanding of the natural order. The process of secularization was a historical moment, no less significant than that of the Reformation. It may have begun as a philosophical or an intellectual movement, but it was gradually transmitted to wider circles until it attained key positions of social and political influence through which it came to dominate European society. We know it as the Enlightenment.

Dawson attributes the interpretation of liberalism in religious terms to the work of Rousseau, who became the founder and prophet of the new faith—the religion of democracy. He pleaded the cause of the individual against society, the poor against the rich, the people against the privileged class, the cause of love against convention, and of intuition against the (classical) philosophers. Dawson credits Thomas Paine with bringing to America the confused ideas of Rousseau and the liberal Protestantism of eighteenth-century Geneva. Paine was the author of *Common Sense*, a pamphlet that came off the press on January 10, 1776, and sold more than 500,000 copies within a few months. It became the articulation of a kind of revolutionary creed. Paine had transformed a local quarrel in Massachusetts concerning taxation and colonial rights into a crusade for the rights of man and the cause of humanity, calling in messianic terms for "a new world order."

In the victory of the American Revolution, European liberals saw the justification of their ideals and the realization of their hopes. In Dawson's judgment, it gave an intellectual current, a political direction, and infused a revolutionary purpose into the democratic idealism of Rousseau. The agrarian democracy of the age of Jefferson—which prevailed at the American founding—was transformed, first by Andrew Jackson and later, more fundamentally, by the vast migration from Europe in the nineteenth century, which prepared the way for the mass democracy we know today.

Dawson's narrative continues. The defeat of national socialism in the Second World War left the modern world divided into two opposing ideologies and political systems: the Communist World and the Western World. The latter is essentially pluralistic and multiform in political power, in ideology, and in industrial and technological planning. But the progress of technology demands a certain degree of international cooperation and internal social unity. A free society requires a degree of spiritual unity more than a totalitarian one. Dawson concludes that the power of the West to withstand communist totalitarianism depended not so much on its military power as it does on cultural leadership: "It is to Christianity that western culture must look for leadership and help in restoring the moral and spiritual unity of our civilization."[6]

As a result of his many books and lectures, Dawson became recognized as one of the foremost cultural historians of his day. It is my conviction that few contemporary historians and social commentators possess both his sweeping knowledge and depth of judgment. Dawson began his teaching career at University College, Exeter, and at the University of Liverpool, after studies at Oxford. He ended that career as the Stillman Professor of Roman Catholic Studies at Harvard University.

---

6. Dawson, 147.

## ❧23❧
# George Santayana and Walter Lippmann

IN SPEAKING OF THE INTELLECTUAL TEMPER of his time, George Santayana in 1913 wrote on the opening page of his *The Winds of Doctrine*: "The shell of Christendom is broken. The unconquerable mind of the East, the pagan past, the industrial socialistic future confront it with their equal authority. Our whole life and mind is saturated with the slow upward filtration of a new spirit—that of an emancipated, atheistic, international democracy."[1]

One of Santayana's students was Walter Lippmann, who served for a time as his student assistant. Walter completed his work for a BA in 1909 in what some consider to be the golden age of Harvard University's faculty of philosophy. It was the period of Josiah Royce, William James, George Santayana, and Alfred North Whitehead. Then too, Freud in distant Vienna was very much in vogue in Boston.

In his early professional career, Lippman found the mild socialist philosophy of his former mentor compelling. Breaking from later radical positions, Lippman was eventually to become, like Santayana, a defender of what may be called a classical philosophical outlook. It is Lippmann's *A Preface to Morals* that I wish to call attention to as we debate the future of higher education in the United States. Written in 1929 and reissued in

---

1. George Santayana, *Winds of Doctrine: Studies in Contemporary Opinion* (London: J. M. Dent and Sons, 1913), 1.

a revised edition in 1952, it is even more relevant today than when it was initially produced. His account of the political conflict of his day is duplicated in today's political climate.

A prolific writer, Lippmann became a syndicated columnist in 1931. His commentary was carried by 250 newspapers in the United States alone. Early books were entitled *A Preface to Politics* (1913), *Drift and Mastery* (1914), *Public Opinion* (1922), *The Good Society* (1937), and *Essays in Public Philosophy* (1955).

In *Public Opinion*, Lippmann seemed to imply that ordinary citizens are incapable of rationally responding to public issues. The mass media, he claimed, produced slogans to which the voting public was likely to respond without any real knowledge of the issues. He eventually came to doubt the possibility of a true democracy. No amount of charters, direct primaries, or shot ballots will make a democracy out of an illiterate people. A person who reads one corrupt newspaper and goes out to vote cannot claim to have registered his will. He may have a will, but he has not used it.

Speaking of the U.S. Constitution, he wrote, "Is there in all the world a more plain-spoken attempt to contrive an automatic governance—a machine which would preserve its balance without the need of taking human nature into account?"[2]

Radicals or utopia makers who wish to substitute some other kind of machine for the one we have don't really believe in what they propose. They may claim that if we put the country under a new political system then human affairs would run automatically for the welfare of all, but it is power they seek.

The quest for power upsets all mechanical foresight and gravitates to the natural leaders. Successful politicians are those

---

2. Walter Lippmann, *A Preface to Politics* (New York: Mitchell Kennerley, 1913), 14.

who know how to tap into public needs and give voice to the common people. The inherent logic and intellectual respectability of any particular policy is less important than its ability to arouse emotions and express the deep feelings of a constituency. "No genuine politician ever treats his constituents as reasoning animals."[3] The successful politician knows that "it is more important to know what the socialist leaders, stump speakers, and pamphleteers think Marx meant than to know what Marx actually said."[4] "The successful politician, good or bad, deals with dynamics, with the will, the hopes, the needs, and visions of men."[5] Those visions pertain to the here and now.

It is important to recognize that "politics is not concerned with prescribing the ultimate qualities of life. When it tries to do so by sumptuary legislation, nothing but mischief is invoked. Its business is to provide opportunities, not to announce ultimate values."[6]

Other dictums will resonate with the contemporary reader. "There is no contradiction in speaking of 'human nature' while admitting that men are unique."[7] Common likeness admits of individual variation. "Human nature is a rather shocking affair if you come to it with ordinary romantic optimism."[8]

Lippmann finds that in America "both art and politics exist in a condition of unnatural celibacy.... A lively artistic or cultural tradition is essential to the humanizing of political differences."[9] "It is enough that we remember the close alliance

3. Lippman, 217.
4. Lippman, 237.
5. Lippman, 217.
6. Lippman, 201.
7. Lippman, 109.
8. Lippman, 39.
9. Lippman, 113.

of art, science and politics in Athens, in Florence and Venice."[10]

"When Christian Churches turn to civics, to reformism or socialism, they are in fact announcing that the Christian dream is dead. They may continue to practice some of its moral teachings and hold to some of its creed, but the Christian impulse is for them no longer active."[11] Lippman develops this claim in a subsequent volume, *A Preface to Morals* (1929), where he adopts William James's utilitarian view of religion.

Toward the end of the volume, Lippman says of his own early twentieth century period, "A political revolution is in progress: the state as policeman is giving place to the state as producer."[12]

Times may change but human nature does not. The passages cited and Lippmann's comments are offered for the insight they provide for our own troubled times. *A Preface to Politics* is well worth revisiting.

10. Lippman, 129.
11. Lippman, 231.
12. Lippman, 271.

# ⁂24⁂
# John T. Scott on Rousseau

JOHN T. SCOTT IS A PROFESSOR of political science at the University of California, Davis. He has previously edited or translated the major political writings of Rousseau. The present volume is not a straightforward narrative of Rousseau's thought but is instead an almost line-by-line textual study of the major works—or should I say influential works—of Rousseau. Scott is mainly interested in the rhetorical and literary strategies Rousseau employs to present his thought. Assessment of that thought varies.

Bertrand Russell, in his *History of Western Philosophy*, was willing to call Rousseau a philosopher in the eighteenth-century French sense but, says Russell, he was not what we would call a philosopher. Judith Shklar, the distinguished Harvard University professor of philosophy, would agree. In her *Men and Citizens: A Study of Rousseau's Social Theory*, she writes: "Jean-Jacques Rousseau was not a professional philosopher. He never pretended that he was. His great claim was that he alone [among his contemporaries] had been 'the painter of nature and the historian of the human heart.'"[1] Jacques Maritain in his *Three Reformers* presents him as a spiritual writer in the mold of Luther and Calvin. Call him what you will, Rousseau's influence was great and lasting, leading immediately to Karl Marx and Vladimir Lenin.

---

1. Judith N. Shklar, *Men and Citizens: A Study of Rousseau's Social Theory* (Cambridge: Cambridge University Press, 1969), 1.

*Rousseau's Reader*, apart from an introduction and a conclusion, consists of seven chapters. Four are devoted to Emile, and the others are entitled, "Discourse on the Sciences and the Arts," "Discourse on Inequality," and "Reading the Social Contract."

A pervading theme in Rousseau's many writings is that man is naturally good; it is our institutions—our social systems—that have made him wicked. The goodness of nature is self-evident from the order one finds in the natural world. "'Everything is good, as it leaves the hands of the Author of things, everything degenerates in the hands of man.' . . . But the alleged goodness of human nature is not so evident," given that civic education has denatured man by transforming him into a being who is consequentially defined only by his citizenship."[2]

"Political rights," Rousseau will say in *The Social Contract*, derive not from nature but are founded on conventions. The nature of those conventions is determined by their purpose.

Whereas Aristotle held that man is by nature a political animal, and furthermore that the polis is a natural condition for human fulfilment, Rousseau emphatically denies both claims and declares to the contrary: "The political community itself is the product of an act of the will, a conventional body created for certain purposes. . . . When men in a state of nature encounter obstacles to their self-preservation, they must form an association productive of a moral order."[3]

As Scott points out, "The social contract is not an act in the sense of an action that actually took place . . . but is instead what I might call a 'principle' related to the very nature of the polit-

---

2. John T. Scott, *Rousseau's Reader: Strategies of Persuasion and Education* (Chicago: University of Chicago Press, 2020), 133.
3. Scott, 269.

ical as such."⁴ The "general will" when declared "is an act of sovereignty and constitutes law." If it is "merely a particular will, or an act of magistracy, it is at most a decree."⁵ Thus, Rousseau distinguishes "the general will from the 'will of all,' which is the sum of the political wills of the members generally."⁶ Laws enacted by the sovereign people "are necessarily general in form and application."⁷ The will of all is just a collection of private wills. The general will reflects the common good and what is best for all. The general will presupposes the existence of a generally accepted political and social ideal. As Scott points out, it is most often associated with socialist traditions in modern politics.

Rousseau will argue that freedom and authority are not contradictory since legitimate laws are founded on the general will of the citizens. In obeying the law, the individual citizen is thus obeying himself as a member of the political community, exercising his personal freedom. Again, the purpose of Rousseau's social contract was to dissolve the state. The civilized state, a product of the arts and science, is responsible for moral degeneration and alienation of people from the mainstream of society. Why does Brussels come to mind?

*Rousseau's Reader* may have been written primarily with a professional audience in mind, yet its relevance to the political world in the year of its publication could not have escaped its author. John T. Scott is to be thanked for this in-depth study, which can be read with profit by the lay reader, as well as the professional philosopher.

---

4. Scott, 269.
5. Rousseau, *The Social Contract*, II.2, translated and cited in Scott, 271.
6. Scott, 271, citing *Social Contract*, II.3.
7. Scott, 272.

## ∻25∾
# Pierre Manent on Montaigne

AFTER A BRIEF INTRODUCTION, Manent begins a chapter-by-chapter analysis of Montaigne's *Essays*. But it is more than that: Manent finds in the *Essays* lessons for today. The book is divided into four parts. Part One is titled "The War of Human Beings." Chapter One is "To Save One's Life."

The stage has already been set by Paul Seaton, who in an informative preface provides an overview of Manent's intellectual journey from his early years under the influence of Leo Strauss to the present. Seaton traces the origin of Manent's interest in the failure of Europe to defend itself to his 1982 publication, *Tocqueville and the Nature of Democracy*. That was followed by *Metamorphoses of the City: On the Dynamism of Western Civilization* in 2010, and in 2017 by the prestigious Étienne Gilson Lecture delivered at L'Institut Catholique de Paris and published the following year as *La loi naturelle et les droits de l'homme*. At present, Manent conducts an ongoing seminar on Aristotle's *Nicomachean Ethics* as a professor at L'École des Haute Études en Sciences Sociales.

In chapter after chapter, the question looms large: what has happened to Europe that it lacks the will to defend its cultural heritage? Has Western civilization exhausted itself, as some have claimed? Manent responds: "In servitude and misery, our forebears conceived the hopes of science and power, of liberty and happiness, on which we have lived during three or four centuries."[1] What happened?

---

1. Pierre Manent, *Montaigne: Life without Law* (Notre Dame: University of Notre Dame Press, 2020), 1.

Seaton explains, "toward the end of the Cold War," Manent noticed "a 'worrisome' depoliticization and attendant 'denationalization' of life and thought in Western Europe."[2] He rose to become the European Union's foremost critic. He criticized the EU's "Idea of Humanity" as "*virtually* integrated" with "no *significant* collective differences" as, in Seaton's words, "patently false and politically debilitating."[3] He instead began to defend a recognition of the nation-state against the internationalists and multiculturalists. Seaton explains that for Manent, "the West could be rendered intelligible" only if one takes into consideration "distinct forms of human association. . . . the city, the empire, and the nation, with the Christian Church."[4] The Church, for Manent, is an important form of "authoritative human association," one both "enriching" and indeed "complicating" the social order.[5]

Luther and Calvin at the beginning of the sixteenth century, in their break with Rome, decisively changed the role of the Church in society. The priesthood of the faithful entailed the rejection of the ordained priesthood and *sola scriptura* placed each believer on his own before the saving Word of God. The Catholic Church, theretofore the mediator between human beings and the divine, was decisively excluded from its role of providing spiritual guidance. Historians generally agree that the Reformation ended the Middle Ages and prepared the way for modernity. Or put another way, Luther's revolt had the effect of gradually transforming Europe from a world per-

2. Seaton, "Translator's Foreword," *Life without Law*, vii.

3. Seaton, vii. The source for the brief quotations from Manent is unclear; several works are mentioned in Seaton's footnote.

4. Seaton, viii.

5. Seaton, viii.

meated by Christianity to one in which religion would be separated from public life.

Speaking of the relief of our wretched human condition, Manent separates Montaigne from the Greek perspective, as well as from the Christian perspective. For Greek philosophy, it is a question of perfecting our nature, of directing our human endowment to its natural end. For Christians it is a question of healing our nature (wounded by sin), that is, to consent to its healing by grace, which alone suffices. For Montaigne, "rather, it is a power of transforming, or of transforming itself.... It is not a matter of rediscovering and actualizing an underlying order, but of giving form to something that does not have form or can take on a thousand forms."[6]

In another interesting passage, Manent observes that Montaigne "claims the liberty to judge princes after their death."[7] "This is the only way," he maintains, "of reconciling respect for 'the political order'—establishing the obedience due to the office of the prince, whether he be good or bad—and the freedom of judgment."[8] The populace must have this freedom to judge, without which there can be no recognition of a just order, broken though it may be.

Manent first quotes the last page of the *Essays*, including this line from Montaigne: "Between ourselves, these are two things that I have always observed to be in singular accord, supercelestial thoughts and subterranean conduct."[9] Manent comments, "Man is the speaking animal, and he is the acting animal.... One can bring action closer to or move it further

---

6. Manent, *Life without Law*, 24.
7. Manent, 15.
8. Manent, 15.
9. Montaigne, cited in Manent, *Life without Law*, 3.

from speech, and the same with speech vis-à-vis action."[10] Hence the need for law. "Laws draw their authority, Montaigne explains," not merely from their written form but "from possession and usage."[11] In themselves, that is, in their birth or their beginnings, they are not much. Laws achieve their authority through their usage and the function they perform.

The greater part of Chapter Eight, "Governed Human Beings," is devoted to Pascal, who addresses a Europe that seems to have abandoned a universal criterion of human action, a natural law or concept of justice capable of guiding the legislator. Manent observes, "With the exception of those who still subscribed to the Thomistic tradition . . . all the authors" of the time including Montaigne and Pascal "abandoned, or rather, explicitly rejected, every idea of an objective human good, a good that could be discerned as such by human reason and on which, consequently, people could agree."[12] Does this situation remain in force?

*Montaigne: Life without Law* may have been written primarily with professional philosophers in mind, but in spite of its at times demanding character, it is accessible to the informed layman. Manent is not writing in a vacuum; his Montaigne offers many lessons for our troubled present.

10. Manent, 3.
11. Manent, 214.
12. Manent, 175.

## ≈26≈
# Niki Kasumi Clements on John Cassian and Christian Ethical Formation

THE BOOK OPENS with an account of a well-educated young man, John Cassian and his companion Germanus, who attempt to establish in Bethlehem a monastic community based on the asceticism of the Egyptian desert model.[1]

The mid-decades of the fifth century have been described by Robert Markus as the watershed of the great debates in the Latin West on what it means to be and live as a Christian. There is ample evidence to support that judgment as we follow the writing and activity of John Cassian, St. Augustine, John Chrysostom, Benedict of Nursia, and Pope Innocent I.

John Cassian, who lived from 360 to 436, was born in what is now Romania. A contemporary of St. Augustine (354–430), he, like Augustine, was led to address the issue of self-formation. Clements observes: "Orienting one's life toward the proximate goal of 'purity of heart' (*puritas cordis*) and the ultimate end of 'the kingdom of God,' Cassian recognizes, is not easy."[2] Neither is answering the question: How much is to be attributed to one's own agency as distinct from the grace of God?

Augustine spoke to the problem in his *On Grace and Free Will* (426), where he stressed human fallenness and human inability. Cassian in *Conference 15*, "On God's Protection," was thought

---

1. Niki Kasumi Clements, *Sites of the Ascetic Self: John Cassian and Christian Ethical Formation* (Notre Dame: University of Notre Dame Press, 2020).
2. Clements, 44.

to offer "a direct response to Augustine and his followers, despite its likely antecedent composition."[3] Cassian's position, which later became known as Semi-Pelagianism, differed from Augustine's insofar as Cassian feared that the doctrine of Augustine possessed an element of fatalism. "We must take care not to refer all the merits of the saints to the Lord in such a way as to ascribe nothing but what is perverse to human nature."[4] Cassian claimed that the initial step to salvation was within the power of the individual unaided by grace. God created humans with a good will, and when human effort fosters this will, God encourages its growth and spurs it on to salvation, increasing what He Himself had planted and saw arise from individual effort. Cassian states that human progress in ascetic formation requires adaptation, as well as human toil and effort, and he notes that divine protection goes "together not with a lazy or careless person but with the one who labors and toils."[5]

Cassian brought to his early works a knowledge of Egyptian asceticism and of the desert hermits. This is seen in his *Institutes of Monastic Life* (418) and *Conferences of the Fathers* (419). A third work, *On the Incarnation of the Lord*, was written against the heretic Nestorius at the request of Pope Leo I. That book, considered his master work, took him nearly a decade to write and appeared in 490. Without doubt his collected works influenced the whole of Western monasticism. Benedict in his *Rule* made Cassian's *Conferences* and *Institutes* required reading.

---

3. Clements, 47.

4. John Cassian, *The Conferences, Part II*, in *Nicene and Post-Nicene Fathers: Second Series*, vol. 11, ed. Philip Schaff and Rev. Henry Wallace (Buffalo, N.Y.: Christian Literature Publishing, 1894), 13.12.5, p. 429.

5. *Non otioso neque securo, sed laboranti ac desudanti eam cooperatam*. Cassian, *Conferences*, 13.13.5. Cited in Clements, 75.

In the opinion of Niki Kasumi Clements, "Cassian is remarkable as a translator between Eastern and Western Christianities. He bridges geographies, languages, politics, customs and friends."[6] Notably, he was embraced not only in the West but by eastern Christianity, as evidenced by the fact that his Latin texts were translated into Greek.

Cassian writes about what an ascetic life looks like—materially and performatively—how it feels, and how it is socially transmitted. He emphasizes asceticism as a means of self-cultivation as opposed to self-renunciation."[7] In writing about communal practices, he stresses adaptations and accommodations for different geographies and times—just as he does with individual ascetic formation."[8] He recognizes how subjects are directed by desire but need to be confirmed in their ambition through practice.

Commissioned by Pope Innocent I to work in southern Gaul, Cassian established near Marseilles two monasteries, one for men and one for women. He founded and became the first abbot of the Abbey St. Victor, where he remained for the rest of his life. His foundation for women was known as the Abbey Saint Salvador.

Cassian was ordained a deacon by John Chrysostom, Archbishop of Constantinople, around 404 and ordained a priest in 405. Although Cassian was never formally canonized, St. Gregory the Great regarded him as a saint, and today his feast with an octave is celebrated in Provence on July 23. His name is also found among the saints of the Greek calendar. A reliquary in Marseilles bears the inscription, "St. John Cassian."

6. Clements, 48.
7. Clements, 102–3.
8. Clements, 151.

Niki Kasumi Clements, in introducing the reader to John Cassian, makes some interesting comparisons to Immanuel Kant, Friedrich Nietzsche, Max Weber, and Michael Foucault insofar as they too discuss the role of asceticism—perhaps better understood as "restraint"—in self-governance and self-improvement.

Ms. Clements, it should be noted, is the Watt J. and Lilly G. Jackson Professor of Religion at Rice University. Conversant with the widespread contemporary interest in Cassian, she acknowledges that her subject lends himself to interpretation. And so it was in the fifth and sixth centuries. Pelagius was formally condemned by the Council of Carthage in 418 for an overly generous view of human free will. Augustine's view on divine grace prevailed at the Council of Carthage in 529 and became the standard of orthodox teaching.

## ≈27≈
# Alberto Boixados on Modern Art

ALBERTO BOIXADOS, surveying the art of his day, shows how far art has degenerated in the twentieth century with the emancipation of the artist from tradition. In Paris alone he can offer, for example, the glass pyramid that disrupts the harmony of the Louvre and the Center Pompidou—which was built in an old and noble quarter—disfiguring its streets and skyline. He finds, in examining Picasso's painting and motivation, that there is a short distance from Picasso to Trotsky. Deliberate emancipation from history, he maintains, constitutes a special kind of subversion, theological in its roots and political in its purpose. Chapters of *Myths of Modern Art* are devoted to painting, music, literature, and the theater, with a special chapter on Central American literature and another focusing on then popular English and American writers—James Joyce, Lionel Trilling, Graham Green, Saul Bello, Ralph Ellison, and Flannery O'Connor.

In his discussion of modern art, Boxiados's favorites are Cezanne, Gauguin, and Rodin. He asserts: "The attempt to liberate oneself from the nature of things is to corrupt the spirit. . . . The portraits of Van Gogh are proof that through right perception of the material of life, a great artist can approach the spiritual."[1]

Citing the drift in the art world from Bach to Baez, Rafael to Jackson Pollock, and Milton to Mailer, Boixados remarks that modern authors are ignoring an important aspect of human

---

1. Alberto Boixados, *Myths of Modern Art*, trans. Reed Armstrong and Roxlana Armstrong (Lanham, Md.: University Press of America, 1991), 13.

nature. At the beginning of the twentieth century Wassily Kandinsky broke the last remaining contact with the sacred in art. "Christian faith in the hereafter," Kandinsky contended, "paradoxical as it may sound, was represented in medieval times by figurative art forms."[2] Religion, however, provided a barrier to the absolute abstraction of the image.

Boixados does not hide his contempt for Picasso—for his capacity for destruction. He finds Picasso acknowledging his deception of wealthy patrons who look for the new, the unusual, the original, the extravagant, and the scandalous. Picasso says of his own work: "I have humored these gentlemen with anything that popped into my head, which the less they understood the more they admired." Picasso admits, "[Compared to] Giotto, Titian, Rembrandt, and Goya . . . I am nothing but a public buffoon."

"Thus," writes Boixados, "the confession of a man with a clear vision, who was conscious of what art should be, and of its profound mission. . . . The purpose of art is to reveal what is hidden from basic senses, not to escape reality but to make it intelligible, fully comprehensible by symbolic means."[3] Étienne Gilson has said much the same thing.

In 1955, Gilson gave the A. W. Mellon Lectures in the Fine Arts at the National Gallery of Art in Washington D.C. to capacity audiences. When those lectures were subsequently published as *Painting and Reality,* Gilson dedicated the volume simply "to J.G. / who taught me to understand what I loved."[4] The mid-decades of the last century were the period that wit-

---

2. Wassily Kandinsky, quoted in Boixados, 3.

3. Boixados, 5–6.

4. That is, his daughter Jacqueline Gilson. Étienne Gilson, *Painting and Reality: The A. W. Mellon Lectures in the Fine Arts* (New York: Pantheon, 1957).

nessed the publication of Bernard Berenson's acclaimed *Aesthetics and History*, Jacques Maritain's *Creative Intuition in Art and Poetry*, and Joseph Pieper's *Leisure: The Basis of Culture*. Whether Albert Boixados read them or not, they bolster the singular contention of the present volume.

To add to his broad study of Western art, Boixados devotes a chapter to "Aspects of Central American Literature." He focuses on the work of Ernesto Cardenal, a priest, writer, and poet, whom he regards as a key to understanding the spiritual dimension of Marxism in Latin America. Cardenal was the beneficiary of a Jesuit high school education. He subsequently studied at the University of Mexico and at Columbia University in New York. In 1957 he joined the Trappists at the Abbey of Gethsemani in Kentucky, made famous by fellow poet Thomas Merton. After two years he left Gethsemani and joined the Benedictines in Cuernavaca. That Benedictine community was subsequently dissolved by the Holy See when it proved to be "a center of Marxist indoctrination of priests and seminarians who went from there to preach in various Latin American countries."[5] Ivan Illich was the most notorious member of the community.

In 1972, Cardenal published a work under the title, *La santidad de revolución* ["The Sanctity of Revolution"], a series of questions to which he provided answers. Concerning the Cuban revolution, he writes, "For me the Cuba experience was truly a revelation. I realize that Marxism is the solution, the only solution, for Latin America."[6] To the question, "What are the essential features of the new man that the socialist countries are trying to create?" he responds, "The new man is a man

---

5. Boixados, *Myths of Modern Art*, 79.
6. Ernesto Cardenal, *La santidad de la revolución*, 2nd ed. (Salamanca: Ediciones Sigueme, 1978), 27.

divested of egotism, a man who lives for the sake of others, to serve the rest."[7]

He adds, "Christianity itself is not a religion but the practice of love, the realization of human fraternity. That is the true religion of Christianity." Religious forms belong to primitive societies. "The rites, the liturgy, the religious forms which serve this purpose, and in this sense can be good, but if they do not serve this purpose, they do not interest us. . . . Popular religion, the processions and devotions of the people can serve liberation. But the moment will come when the people will outgrow this religious stage."[8] At the time this book was written, Cardenal had become the spiritual guide to the Marxist Sandinista in Nicaragua, serving as its Minister of Culture.

Pope Francis is no stranger to this intellectual milieu. It may have subtly contributed to his own formation. Those who followed John Paul II's visit to Nicaragua on television saw him publicly chide Cardenal, who was suspended from the priesthood. Pope Francis removed the then-94-year-old Cardenal's canonical censures in 2019.

Tribute must be paid to Reed and Roxlana Armstrong, both artists, for their early introduction of Alberto Boixados to an English-speaking audience. The book is perhaps more relevant today than when it was written thirty years ago. The late Reed Armstrong may be cited as the foremost sculptor of religious art in North America. His website with photographs of many of his works will bear this out. Roxlana Armstrong is both a writer and a painter, who continues her work in Front Royal, Virginia.

7. Cardenal, 31.
8. Cardenal, 41.

# ∞28∞
# Impossibility of a View from Nowhere

"THE VIEW FROM NOWHERE" is a phrase made famous by Thomas Nagel in a book he published in 1986 by that name.[1] Nagel spoke of the negative effect of reporting that claimed to be neutral, where opposing views or persons are granted equal validity or deemed equally worthy of a hearing. Supposed impartiality is believed to give the "balanced" report universal or moral legitimacy, denied to anyone who dares to defend a particular point of view.

Failure to recognize truth in the pursuit of impartiality is particularly egregious in discussions of sexual morality. Pretending that a homosexual union is morally equivalent to a procreative union prevents one from addressing the question of the good or purpose of sexual activity. Aristotle reminds us that to promote good conduct is to explain its purpose. To judge is normally regarded as an assessment made from a perspective. Judged in terms of purpose, the value of homosexual activity—like other forms of hedonism—is suspect. Purpose, it can be said, is written into the laws of nature.

Viewed from a historical perspective, the sanctions that the nation once habitually acknowledged have long been eroded by the acid of modernity. As Walter Lippman observed, "an authoritative code of morals has force and

---

1. Thomas Nagel, *The View from Nowhere* (New York: Oxford University Press, 1989).

effect only when it expresses the settled customs of a stable society."²

It is a Christian perspective, specifically a Catholic perspective, that I wish to talk about. The Ten Commandments, which used to be displayed prominently in primary schools throughout the nation, antedate Christianity and are rightly a component of Catholic moral teaching; so too is much of Stoic moral teaching. The Church, it may be said, has not so much produced a common morality as it has endorsed the highest moral principles acknowledged by mankind. That morality, suffused with the teachings of Christ, is expressed in His words: "I am the Way, the Truth, and the Life" (Jn 14:6).

In speaking of a Christian point of view I am reminded of Dorothy Sayers's magnificent 1947 Oxford University address, "The Lost Tools of Learning." In it, available on several sites on the internet, she speaks of the order in which education in the important things should be advanced. Children at an early age should be taught Greek and Latin. "At the grammatical age, therefore, [they] should become acquainted with the story of God and Man in outline—i.e., the Old and New Testament presented as parts of a single narrative of Creation, Rebellion, and Redemption—and also with 'the Creed, the Lord's Prayer, and the Ten Commandments.' At this stage, it does not matter nearly so much that these things should be fully understood as that they should be known and remembered."³ The grammatical stage is followed by the second and

---

2. Walter Lippmann, *A Preface to Morals*, Chapter 15 in *The Essential Lippmann: A Political Philosophy for Liberal Democracy*, ed. Clinton Rossiter and James Laire (Cambridge, Mass.: Harvard University Press), 482.

3. Dorothy L. Sayers, "The Lost Tools of Learning," lecture given at Oxford University, 1947.

third parts of the trivium, that of logic and rhetoric. It is in the logical stage that the pupil learns mathematics, algebra, geometry, and the more advanced form of mathematics. Logic, Sayers's notes, has been discredited "partly because we have fallen into the habit of supposing that we are conditioned almost entirely by the intuitive and the unconscious."[4] At the rhetorical stage the student will find that logic is the art of correctly organizing an argument.

An egregious example of the failure to place things in a proper perspective is found in the recent action of the curators of New York's Metropolitan Museum of Art as reported by Eric Gibson in the Wall Street Journal. Under the title, "Museum at a Crossroads," Gibson tells us that a visitor to the museum will now read at the entrance to a celebratory exhibit—"Making the Met, 1817–2020"—that "the museum's founders hailed 'from White Protestant and New York society,'" as if that were an important factor. Gibson comments: "Ominous are the indications that the Met's leadership has bought into the notion of museums as dens of inequity in need of a makeover and plans to replace the old, universalist model with an ideological, sectarian approach to its collections and exhibitions."[5]

Whether that proves to be so or not remains to be seen. The point I am making is that the Met's collection did not arise from nowhere but developed in a cultural context beautifully described by Dorothy Sayers. Toward the end of her essay, Sayers makes another well-known observation worth repeating: "Many people to-day who are atheist or agnostic in religion, are governed by in their conduct by a code of Christian

---

4. Sayers.
5. Eric Gibson, "'Making the Met, 1870–2020' Review: Museum at a Crossroads," *Wall Street Journal*, November 4, 2020.

ethics which is so rooted in their unconscious assumptions that it never occurs to them to question it.

"But one cannot live on capital forever. A tradition, however firmly rooted, if it is never watered, though it dies hard, yet in the end it dies."[6]

---

6. Sayers, "The Lost Tools of Learning."

# Bibliography

Allers, Rudolph. *The Successful Error: A Critical Study of Freudian Psychoanalysis*. New York: Sheed and Ward, 1940.

Aquinas, Thomas. *Summa Contra Gentiles*. Translated by Anton C. Pegis. Garden City, N.Y.: Random House, 1961.

Atkins, Richard Kenneth. *Peirce and the Conduct of Life: Sentiment and Instincts in Ethics and Religion*. Cambridge: Cambridge University Press, 2016.

Bacon, Francis. "Aphorisms Concerning the Interpretation of Nature and the Kingdom of Man." In *The Works of Francis Bacon*. Edited by Douglas Denon Heath, James Spedding, and Robert Leslie Ellis. London: Longmans, 1858.

———. *Novum Organum: Aphorismi de interpretatione naturae et regno hominis*. Edited by W. Krohn. Darmstadt: Wissenschaftlich Buchgesellschaft, 1990.

Bark, W. C. *Origins of the Medieval World*. New York: Doubleday, 1960.

Barnes, Jonathan. *Aristotle*. Oxford: Oxford University Press, 1989.

Benedict XVI, Pope. "Address to the Meeting with Representatives from the Worlds of Culture and the Economy (Venice)." May 8, 2011.

Ben-Menahem, Yemima. *Causation in Science*. Princeton, N.J.: Princeton University Press, 2018.

Berquist, Richard. *From Human Dignity to Natural Law*. Washington, D.C.: The Catholic University of America Press, 2019.

Blankart, Charles B., and Dennis C. Miller, eds. *A Constitution for the European Union*. Cambridge, Mass.: MIT Press, 2004.

Boixados, Alberto. *Myths of Modern Art*. Translated by Reed Armstrong and Roxlana Armstrong. Lanham, Md.: University Press of America, 1991.

Brague, Rémi. *The Legend of the Middle Ages: Philosophical Explorations of Medieval Christianity, Judaism, and Islam*. Translated by Lydia G. Cochrane. Chicago: University of Chicago Press, 2009.

———. *The Legitimacy of the Human*. Translated by Paul Seaton. South Bend, Ind.: St. Augustine Press, 2018.

———. "On the Need for a Philosophy of Nature and on Aquinas's Help in Sketching One." *Proceedings of the American Catholic Philosophical Association* 89 (2015): 35–43.

Cardenal, Ernesto. *La santidad de la revolución*, 2nd ed. Salamanca: Ediciones Sigueme, 1978.

Carroll, Lewis. *Alice's Adventures in Wonderland and Through the Looking-Glass*. New York: Bantam Dell, 1981.

Cassian, John. *The Conferences, Part II*, in *Nicene and Post-Nicene Fathers: Second Series*, vol. 11. Edited by Philip Schaff and Rev. Henry Wallace. Buffalo, N.Y.: Christian Literature Publishing, 1894.

Chadwick, Owen. *The Making of the Benedictine Ideal*. Washington, D.C.: St. Anselm Abbey, 1981.

Cicero, Marcus Tullius. *De Officiis*. Translated by Walter Miller. Cambridge, Mass.: Harvard University Press, 1913.

———. *De Senectute*, in *Cicero: De Senectute, De Amicitia, De Divinatione.*, Translated by William Armistead Falconer. London: William Heinemann, 1923.

———. "Discussions at Tusculum." In *Cicero, On the Good Life*. Translated by Michael Grant. London: Penguin Books, 1917.

———. *On Duties*. Translated by Walter Miller. Cambridge, Mass.: Harvard University Press, 1997.

Clements, Niki Kasumi. *Sites of the Aesthetic Self: John Cassian and Christian Ethical Formation*. Notre Dame, Ind.: University of Notre Dame Press, 2020.

Comte, Auguste. *On Intellectuals*. Edited by Philip Rieff. Garden City, NY: Doubleday, 1969.

Congdon, Lee. *Solzhenitsyn: The Historical-Spiritual Destinies of Russia and the West*. DeKalb, Ill.: Northern Illinois University Press, 2017.

Corona, Marial. *The Philosophy of John Henry Newman and Pragmatism: A Comparison*. Washington, D.C.: The Catholic University of America Press, 2023.

Crombie, A. C. *Medieval and Early Modern Science*. Garden City, N.Y.: Doubleday, 1959.

Dawson, Christopher. *Dynamics of World History*. Edited by John J. Mulloy. Wilmington, Del.: ISI Books.

———. *The Gods of the Revolution*. Washington, D.C.: The Catholic University of America Press, 2015.

———. *Medieval Essays*. London: Sheed and Ward, 1853.

———. *Religion and the Rise of Western Culture: The Classic Study of Medieval Civilization*. New York: Doubleday, 1991.

Descartes, René. *Discourse on Method and Meditations*. Translated by Elizabeth S. Haldane and G. R. T. Ross. Mineola, N.Y.: Dover, 2003.

Devlin, Lord Patrick. *The Enforcement of Morals*. London: Oxford University Press, 1963.

Dewey, John. *The Collected Works of John Dewey, 1882–1953*. Vol. 1. Edited by Jo A. Boydston. Carbondale: Southern Illinois University Press.

———. *A Common Faith*, 2nd ed. New Haven: Yale University Press, 2013.

———. *Experience and Nature*. New York: W. W. Norton, 1938.

———. *The Quest for Certainty*. New York: Minton Balch, 1929.

Durkheim, Émile. *The Division of Labor*. New York: Free Press, 2014.

———. *The Elementary Forms of Religious Life*. Translated by J. W. Swain. New York: Collier, 1961.

———. *Professional Ethics and Civic Morals*. London: Routledge, 1957.

———. *Rules of Sociological Method*. Glencoe, Ill.: Free Press, 1964.

Dworkin, Ronald. *Taking Rights Seriously*. Cambridge, Mass.: Harvard University Press, 1977.

Farrington, Benjamin. *The Faith of Epicurus*. London: Weidenfield and Nicholson, 1967.

———. *Greek Science*. Harmondsworth, UK: Penguin, 1944.

———. *Science in Antiquity*. London: Oxford University Press, 1967.

Finnis, John. *Aquinas: Moral and Political Theory*. New York: Oxford University Press, 1998.

———. *Natural Law and Natural Rights*. Oxford: Clarendon Press, 1988.

Freud, Sigmund and Ernest Jones. *Complete Correspondence of Sigmund Freud and Ernest Jones, 1908–1939*. Edited by R. Andrew Paskauskas. Cambridge, Mass.: Harvard University Press, 1993.

Gaukroger, Stephen. *The Emergence of a Scientific Culture and the Shaping of Modernity*. Oxford: Clarendon Press, 2006.

Gay, Peter. *The Enlightenment: An Interpretation*. Vol. 1, *The Rise of Modern Paganism*. New York: Publisher, 1966.

Gerson, Lloyd. *Aristotle and Other Platonists*. Ithaca, N.Y.: Cornell University Press, 2005.

Giannozzo, Manetti. *On Human Worth and Excellence*. Edited and translated by Brian P. Copenhaver. Cambridge, Mass.: Harvard University Press, 2019.

Gibson, Eric. "'Making the Met, 1870–2020' Review: Museum at a Crossroads." *Wall Street Journal*, November 4, 2020.

Gilson, Étienne. *Being and Some Philosophers*. 2nd ed. Toronto: Pontifical Institute of Medieval Studies, 1952.

———. *Heloise et Abelard*. Paris: Librairie Philosophie, 1948. English version: *Héloïse et Abélard*. Translated by L. K. Shook. Chicago: Regnery Company, 1951.

———. *Painting and Reality: The A. W. Mellon Lectures in the Fine Arts*. New York: Pantheon, 1957.

Gregory, Brad S. *Rebel in the Ranks: Martin Luther, the Reformation and Conflicts That Continue to Shape Our World*. New York: Harper, 2018.

Groarke, Louis. *An Aristotelian Account of Induction: Creating Something from Nothing*. Montreal: McGill-Queen's University, 2009.

Halbertal, Moshe. *Maimonides: Life and Thought*. Princeton: Princeton University Press, 2014.

Harré, Rom. *The Principles of Scientific Thinking*, ch. 4, "Laws of Nature." Chicago: University of Chicago Press, 1970.

Jackson, Julian. *De Gaulle*. Cambridge, Mass.: Harvard University Press, 2018.

Lippmann, Walter. *A Preface to Politics*. New York: Mitchell Kennerley, 1913.

Loisy, Alfred. *L'évangile et l'église*. Bellevue: Chez l'auteur, 1904.

Luther, Martin. "Disputation against Scholastic Theology." In *Luther's Works*. Edited by Helmut T. Lehmann. Vol. 31, *Career of the Reformer: I*, edited by Harold J. Grimm. Philadelphia: Muhlenberg Press, 1957.

———. *Reformation Writings of Martin Luther*. Vol I, translated by Bertram Lee Wolf. London: Butterworth Press, 1952.

Mackie, John Leslie. *Cement of the Universe: A Study of Causation*. Oxford: Clarendon Press, 1974.

Madison, James. *The Papers of James Madison*. Edited by William T. Hutchinson and William M. E. Rachals. Chicago: University of Chicago Press, 1962.

Mahdi, Muhsin S. "Islamic Theology and Philosophy." In *Encyclopaedia Britannica*, 15th ed.

Maimonides, Moses. *The Guide of the Perplexed*. Translated by Shlomo Pines. Chicago: Chicago University Press, 1974.

Manent, Pierre. *Montaigne: Life without Law*. Translated by Paul Seaton. Notre Dame, Ind.: University of Notre Dame Press, 2020.

Manetti, Giannozzo. *On Human Worth and Excellence*. Edited and translated by Brian P. Copenhaver. I Tatti Renaissance Library. Cambridge, Mass.: Harvard University Press, 2019.

Maritain, Jacques. *Formal Logic*. Translated by Imelda Choquette. New York: Sheed & Ward, 1937.

———. *Man and the State*. Chicago: University of Chicago Press, 1951.

———. *The Person and the Common Good*. London: Geffory Bles, 1948.

———. *Three Reformers*. London: Sheed and Ward, 1950.

Marx, Karl, and Friedrich Engles. *The Communist Manifesto*. New York: International Publishers, 1935.

Mauriac, Francois. *Bloc-notes,* vol. II: 1958–1960. Paris: Seuil, 1993.

McInerny, Ralph. *Ethica Thomistica*. Washington, D.C.: The Catholic University of America Press, 1962.

Mearsheimer, John J. *The Great Delusion: Liberal Dreams and International Realities*. New Haven: Yale University Press, 2018.

Mill, John Stuart. *Nature and Utility of Religion*. New York: The Liberal Arts Press, 1958.

———. *Principles of Political Economy*. Oxford: Oxford University Press, 1994.

Miller, Fred. *Nature, Justice, and Rights in Aristotle's Politics*. Oxford: Clarendon Press, 1995.

*Mitchell v. Couch*, 285 S.W.2d 901 (Ky. Ct. App. 1955).

Moore, Ruth. *Neils Bohr: The Man, His Science and the World They Changed*. Cambridge Mass.: MIT Press, 1985.

Murray, Charles. "Measuring Achievement: The West and the Rest." American Enterprise Institute. August 6, 2003. https://www.aei.org/articles/measuring-achievement/.

Murray, John Courtney. *We Hold These Truths*. New York: Sheed and Ward, 1960.

Murray, Rosalind. *The Good Pagan's Failure*. New York: Longmans, Green, and Co., 1948.

Nagel, Thomas. *The View from Nowhere*. New York: Oxford University Press, 1989.

Newman, John Henry. *Historical Studies II*. London: Longmans, Green, and Co., 1973.

———. "The Nature of Faith in Relation to Reason." In *Fifteen Sermons Preached before the University of Oxford between A.D. 1826 and 1843*. London: Longmans, Green, and Co., 1900.

Nietzsche, Friedrich. *Twilight of the Gods*. In *Portable Nietzsche*. Translated by Walter Kaufmann. New York: Penguin, 1976.

Peirce, Charles Sanders. "A Neglected Argument for the Reality of God." *Hibbert Journal* 7, no. 90 (1908).

Pieper, Joseph. *Scholasticism: Personalities and Problems in Medieval Philosophy*. London: Faber and Faber, 1960.

Pipes, Richard. *Property and Freedom*. New York: Alfred A. Knopf, 1999.

Pocock, J. G. A. *The Machiavellian Moment: Florentine Political Thought and the Atlantic Republican Tradition*. Princeton: Princeton University Press, 1975.

Popkin, Jeremy D. *A New World Begins: The History of the French Revolution*. New York: Basic Books, 2019.

Quine, William. *The Roots of Reference*. LaSalle, Ill.: Open Court, 1974.

Rawls, John. *The Law of Peoples: With the Idea of Public Reason Revisited*. Cambridge, Mass.: Harvard University Press, 1999.

———. *A Theory of Justice*. Cambridge, Mass.: Harvard University Press, 1971.

Rist, John M. *Real Ethics*. Cambridge, Mass.: Cambridge University Press, 2002.

———. *What Is a Person? Realities, Realities, Constructs, Illusions*. Cambridge: Cambridge University Press, 2020.

Robinson, Daniel. *Aristotle's Psychology*. New York: Columbia University Press, 1989.

Robson, Roy R. *Old Believers in Modern Russia*. DeKalb, Ill.: Northern Illinois University Press, 1995.

Royce, Josiah. "Before and since Kant." *The Berkely Quarterly* 2 (January 1881): 134.

Russell, Bertrand. *Religion and Science*. London: Allen and Unwin, 1935.

Ryle, Gilbert. *The Concept of Mind*. Introduction by Daniel C. Dennett. Chicago: University of Chicago Press, 2002.

Saint-Exupéry, Antoine de. *Ecrits de guerre, 1939–1944*. Paris: Gallimard, 1982.

Saliba, George. *Islamic Science and the Making of the European Renaissance*. Cambridge, Mass.: MIT Press, 2007.

Sandel, Michael J. *Democracy's Discontent*. Cambridge, Mass.: Harvard University Press, 1996.

Santayana, George. *The Idea of Christ in the Gospels*. New York: Charles Scribner's Sons, 1946.

———. *Interpretations of Poetry and Religion*. New York: Charles Scribner's Sons, 1900.

———. *Winds of Doctrine: Studies in Contemporary Opinion*. London: J. M. Dent and Sons, 1913.

Sayers, Dorothy. "The Lost Tools of Learning," lecture given at Oxford University, 1947.

Scammell, Michael, ed. *The Solzhenitsyn Files*. Translated by Catherine A. Fitzpatrick et al. Chicago: Edition Q, 1995.

Scheler, Max. *Schriften zur Anthropologie*. Edited by M. Arndt. Stuttgart: Reclam, 1994.

Scott, John T. *Rousseau's Reader: Strategies of Persuasion and Education*. Chicago: University of Chicago Press, 2020.

Sharkey, Sarah Borden. *Thine Own Self: Individuality in Edith Stein's Later Writings*. Washington, D.C.: The Catholic University of America Press, 2010.

Sherover, Charles M. *From Kant and Royce to Heidegger: Essays in Modern Philosophy*. Washington, D.C.: The Catholic University of America Press, 2003.

Shklar, Judith N. *Men and Citizens: A Study of Rousseau's Social Theory*. Cambridge: Cambridge University Press, 1969.

Siedentop, Larry. *Inventing the Individual: The Origins of Western Liberalism*. Cambridge, Mass.: Harvard University Press, 2017.

Solzhenitsyn, Aleksandr. *Letter to Soviet Leaders*. Translated by Hilary Sternberg. New York: Harper and Row, 1974.

———. *Solzhenitsyn at Harvard*. Edited by Ronald Berman. Washington, D.C.: Ethics and Public Policy Center, 1980.

———. *Warning to the West*. Translated by Harris L. Coulter and Nataly Martin, edited by Alexis Kimoff. New York: Farrar, Strauss and Giroux, 1976.

Strawson, P. F. *Individuals: An Essay in Descriptive Metaphysics*. London: Methuen, 1959.

Taylor, Charles. *A Secular Age*. Cambridge, Mass.: Harvard University Press, 2007.

Valery, Paul. *Collected Works*. Translated by Denise Folliot and Jackson Matthews. New York: Bollingen Foundation, 1962.

Van Steenbergen, Fernand. *Aristotle in the West*. Louvain: E. Nauwelaerts, 1955.

———. *The Philosophical Movement in the Thirteenth Century*. London: Nelson, 1955.

Washington, George. "Washington's Farewell Address." September 19, 1796. Available at https://www.mountvernon.org/education/primary-sources-2/article/washington-s-farewell-address-1796/.

Watson, James, and Francis Crick. Quoted in "DNA Pioneers Lash Out at Religion." *The Washington Times*. March 24, 2003. https://www.washingtontimes.com/news/2003/mar/24/20030324-090202-5705r/.

White, Lynn, Jr. "Dynamo and Virgin Reconsidered." *The American Scholar* 27, no. 2 (1958): 183–94.

Whitehead, Alfred North. *Science and the Modern World*. New York: Macmillan, 1925.

Wolpert, L. *The Unnatural Nature of Science*. Cambridge, Mass.: Harvard University Press, 1993.

# Index

## A
abduction, 139–40
Abelard, Peter, 115
Abélard of Paris, 63
Adler, Alfred, 11
Allers, Rudolf, 7, 11–14
Ambrose of Milan, 28
analogy, 133–35
Anselm of Canterbury, 114–15
apperception, 12
Aquinas, Thomas, 57, 62–63, 115, 142, 146–47
Archytas of Tarentum, 25
*Aristotelian Account of Induction, An* (Groarke), 140–42
Aristotle, 14, 35, 82, 108; Abélard of Paris and, 63; Averroes and, 62–63; causality and, 104; Church Fathers and, 6, 113; Cicero and, 26; Descartes and, 142; education and, 114; intellectual tradition and, 114–15; Luther and, 55; Maimonides and, 66–69; morality in, 18, 179; potentiality and, 128; science and, 127; soul in, 106; theology and, 147–48
*Aristotle's Theory of Abstraction* (Bach), 141
Armstrong, Reed, 178
Armstrong, Roxlana, 178
art, 129–30, 175–78
asceticism, 171–74
Ash'arites, 69
aspiration, purity in, 87–91
Assad, Bashar al, 120
Athenagoras, 6, 113
Augustine, 26, 28–29, 106, 171–72
authoritarianism, 78
autonomy, 17, 83
Averroes, 62–63, 115
Avicenna, 66

## B
Bach, Allan, 141
Bacon, Francis, 96, 142
Bacon, Roger, 115
Barber, Lionel, 46–48
Benedict of Nursia, 6, 29, 111–12, 172–73
Benedict XVI, Pope, 72–73
Ben-Menahem, Yemina, 101–4
Bentham, Jeremy, 118
Berenson, Bernard, 177
Bernard of Clairvaux, 114
Binswanger, Ludwig, 12
Blok, Alexander, 97
"blue laws," 88
Blumenberg, Hans, 97
Boethius, 81
Boixados, Alberto, 175–78
Bonaventure, 115
Brague, Rémi, 71–72, 95–99, 143–44, 147
Brezhnev, Leonid, 75–76
Bush, George W., 117, 119

## C

Cajetan, 57
Calonne, Charles Alexandre de, 52
Calvin, John, 163, 168
capitalism, 16, 27
Cardenal, Ernesto, 177–78
Cartwright, Thomas, 88
Cassian, John, 171–73
Cassiodorus, 6, 113
causality, 13, 101–2
Chandrasekhar, Subrahmanyan, 103
Charlemagne, 29–30
Chirac, Jacques, 47
Chrysostom, John, 173
Cicero, 23–26, 35, 105, 108
*City of God* (Augustine), 29
Clement of Alexandria, 6, 113
Clements, Niki Kasumi, 171, 173–74
*Common Sense* (Paine), 156
Comte, Auguste, 7, 15, 17, 84, 90
*Concept of Mind, The* (Ryle), 104
*Conferences of the Fathers* (Cassian), 172–73
Congdon, Lee, 75–79
contraception, 39
*Conventionalism: From Poincaré to Quine* (Ben-Menahem), 101
Copenhaver, Brian P., 105
Copernicus, 115, 125
Coser, Lewis, 16
Cote, René, 42
Council of Carthage, 174
Council of Reims, 30
Cowan, Clyde, 126
creation, 98–99, 106
Crick, Francis, 124
crime, 83
Crombie, A. C., 111
cultural identity, 2–3

## D

da Barga, Antonio, 105, 108
Darwin, Charles, 13, 123–24
Davidson, Donald, 104
Dawkins, Richard, 31
Dawson, Christopher, 51, 155–58
*de Anima* (Aristotle), 63, 114
*Decline of the West, The* (Spengler), 2
de Gaulle, Charles, 37–43
dei Segni, Lotario, 108
democracy, 34–36, 39, 118, 156–58
Democritus, 107–8
Descartes, René, 96, 142
*De Senectute (On Old Age)* (Cicero), 23–24
de Vio, Thomas, 57
Devlin, Lord Patrick, 82
Dewey, John, 16, 34, 91, 124–25, 150
Diderot, Denis, 156
"Disputation against Scholastic Theology, A" (Luther), 55–56
diversity, 35
*Divine Institutes, The* (Lactantius), 107
*Division of Labor, The* (Durkheim), 15–16, 19
DNA, 124
Duns Scotus, John, 115, 146
Durkheim, Émile, 15–21, 83–85, 91
Dyer, Mary, 88
"Dynamo and Virgin Reconsidered" (White), 4–5, 111–12

## E

Eade, Philip, 20
*Eccentric Culture* (Brague), 95, 143
Eck, Johann, 58
*Edge of the Sword, The* (de Gaulle), 38
education, 114, 124, 150
Einstein, Albert, 124
*Emergence of a Scientific Culture, The* (Gaukroger), 141
empiricism, 127
*Encyclopédie*, 51–52, 156
Enlightenment, 3–4, 156
entropy, 103–4
Epicurus, 107
Erasmus of Rotterdam, 55
*Être et le néant, L'* (Sartre), 12
*Exsurge Domine* (Leo X), 58

## F

Facio, Bartolomeo, 105
Falconer, William A., 23
"Farewell Address" (Washington), 33–36
Farrington, Benjamin, 5–6, 112–13
Fermi, Enrico, 126
*Finite and Eternal Being* (Stein), 146
Foucault, Michel, 97
Fouché, Joseph, 52
*France and Her Army* (de Gaulle), 38
Francis, Pope, 178
Franco, Francisco, 78
"Freedom of Christianity" (Luther), 59
free will, 13, 61–70, 174
French Revolution, 1, 16, 156
Freud, Sigmund, 11–13

## G

Galileo, 115, 123–25
Gans, Paul, 115
Gaukroger, Stephen, 1, 141
Gell-Mann, Murray, 144–45
Genesis, Book of, 98–99, 106
Gibson, Eric, 180
Gilson, Étienne, 63, 63n4, 142, 176–77
Gobel, Jean-Baptiste, 54
Goethe, Johann Wolfgang, 97
*Good Pagan's Failure, The* (Murray), 45–46
Gorin, Felix, 41
*Great Delusion, The* (Mearsheimer), 117–21
Gregory, Brad S., 55–57, 59
Gregory the Great, 29
Griesinger, Wilhelm, 12
Groarke, Louis, 140–42
Grosseteste, Robert, 115
Grotius, Hugo, 31
*Guide for the Perplexed* (Maimonides), 61, 64–65, 69–70
*Gulag Archipelago, The* (Brezhnev), 76

## H

Halbertal, Moshe, 61–62
Harré, Rom, 133
Harris, William Torrey, 148–49
Hegel, Georg, 11, 150
Heidegger, Martin, 71
Heisenberg, Werner, 124
Hempel, Carl, 126
Hildegard of Bingen, 115
*History of Western Philosophy* (Russell), 163

Hobbes, Thomas, 31, 90
Human Genome Project, 145n10
humanities, 97
Hume, David, 18, 82, 125, 127, 139
Huntington, Samuel P., 2–3, 6
Husserl, Edmund, 2, 146
Hutchison, Anne, 88

**I**

ibn Shoshan, Judah, 64
individuation, 146–47
induction, 139–43
Innocent I, Pope, 173
Innocent III, Pope, 108
*Inventing the Individual: The Origins of Western Liberalism* (Siedentop), 27
Islam, 22, 27, 30–31, 91

**J**

Jackson, Julian, 37, 43
James, William, 139, 149, 162
Jaspers, Karl, 12
Jefferson, Thomas, 35, 158
Jesus Christ, 45, 150, 180
John XXIII, Pope, 39, 43
*Journal of Speculative Philosophy*, 148–49
Judaism, 61–62, 64–66
Jung, Carl, 11–12
Justin Martyr, 6, 113

**K**

Kandinsky, Wassily, 176
Kant, Immanuel, 125, 139, 149
Kauffman, Eric P., 6–7
Kennnan, George, 119

Kepler, Johannes, 115, 125
Kirkpatrick, W. H., 150

**L**

Lactantius, 105
Latin Averroism, 62
Lavoisier, Antoine, 54
law: "blue laws," 88; justice and, 82–83; in Manent, 170; neutrality doctrine and, 90; personhood in, 81–82; Roman, 2
Lefebvre des Noëttes, Richard, 115
*Legend of the Middle Ages, The* (Brague), 71, 143
*Legitimacy of the Modern, The* (Blumenberg), 97
Lenin, Vladimir, 163
Leo I, Pope, 172
Leo X, Pope, 56–57
*Letter to Soviet Leaders* (Congdon), 75
Leucippus, 107–8
Lewis, Michael J., 1, 109
liberalism, 27–28, 30–31, 118–19, 156
Libya, 47
Lippmann, Walter, 159–62, 179–80
Locke, John, 90, 125, 127, 139
Loisy, Alfred, 98
Lombard, Peter, 105
Lonergan, Bernard, 71
Louis XVI of France, 52–54
Lucan, 63
Luther, Martin, 55–59, 163, 168

**M**

MacIntyre, Alasdair, 82
Mackie, J. L., 132

Madison, James, 90
Magnus, Albertus, 115
Maimonides, Moses, 61–70, 115
Malesherbes, Guillaume-Chrétien de Lamoignon de, 53–54
Manent, Pierre, 99, 167–70
Manetti, Giannozzo, 105–8
Mankowski, Paul, 20
Marcel, Gabriel, 11
Maritain, Jacques, 39, 43, 71, 140–43, 146–47, 163, 177
Markus, Robert, 171
Martel, Charles, 29
Marx, Karl, 16, 161, 163
Marxism, 27, 31, 177–78
Mason, George, 21, 89
materialism, 11–12, 78, 84, 150–51
Mauriac, François, 42
May, Rollo, 12
Mearsheimer, John J., 117–21
*Men and Citizens: A Study of Rousseau's Social Theory* (Shklar), 163
*Meno* (Plato), 72
Merton, Thomas, 177
*Metaphysics* (Aristotle), 63, 104, 114
Metropolitan Museum of Art (New York), 180
Meynert, Theodor, 12
Middle Ages, 4–5, 63, 82, 98, 110–11, 168
Mill, John Stuart, 90–91
*Mishneh Torah* (Maimonides), 61–62, 64–65
*Mitchell v. Couch*, 84
Mitterrand, François, 39
models, 133–37

modernity, 11, 14, 55, 97–98, 110, 168, 179
monasteries, 6, 111, 113–14, 172–73
Montaigne, Michel de, 167–70
Monte Casino, 6
Montesquieu, 52
Mounier, Emmanuel, 38
Murray, Gilbert, 45
Murray, Rosalind, 45–46
mystical experience, 65–66

## N

Nagel, Ernest, 126
Nagel, Thomas, 179
"Neglected Argument for the Reality of God, A" (Peirce), 140
neutrality doctrine, 90
Newman, John Henry, 18
Newton, Isaac, 103
*New World Begins, A: The History of the French Revolution* (Popkin), 51, 54
Nietzsche, Friedrich, 11, 155–56
Ninety-Five Theses (Luther), 56
North Korea, 46
Norton, J. D., 101
Notre Dame Cathedral (Paris), 1, 109–10

## O

Obama, Barack, 117, 119–20
*On Human Worth and Excellence* (Manetti), 105–8
*On the God of the Christians and One or Two Others* (Brague), 95
*On the Incarnation of the Lord* (Cassian), 172

*On the Miseries of Human Life* (Innocent III), 108
Ortega y Gasset, José, 11
"Out of Depth" (Waugh), 20–21

## P

Paine, Thomas, 156
*Painting and Reality* (Gilson), 176–77
"Papacy at Rome, The: A Treatise on Good Works" (Luther), 57–58
Pascal, Blaise, 170
Paul, 28, 32
Pauli, Wolfgang, 126
Péguy, Charles, 38
Peirce, Charles Sanders, 18, 139–40, 147
Pelagius, 174
Penn, William, 88
Percy, Walker, 71
personalism, 38, 146
personhood, 81–85
physics, 123–37, 143–44. *See also* science
*Physics* (Aristotle), 63, 114, 143
Picasso, Pablo, 176
Pieper, Josef, 63, 177
Pines, Shlomo, 69
Plato, 6, 14, 26, 72, 106, 113
Pocock, J. G. A., 16
Popkin, Jeremy D., 51–54
Popper, Karl, 125
populism, 15
Porphyry, 96, 106
positivism, 7, 17, 21, 125–26
potentiality, 128–29

*Praise of Folly* (Erasmus of Rotterdam), 55
*Preface to Morals, A* (Lippmann), 159–60, 162
Protestantism, 59. *See also* Luther, Martin; Reformation
Psichari, Ernest, 146
psychoanalysis, 11–13
*Psychology of Character, The* (Allers), 11
*Public Opinion* (Lippmann), 160
Puritans, 59, 87–89
purity, in aspiration, 87–91
Putin, Vladimir, 46–48
Putnam, Hilary, 104
Pythagoras, 96, 106

## Q

quantum mechanics, 102–4

## R

Rahner, Karl, 71
Ratzinger, Joseph, 72–73
realism, 101, 118–19, 121, 125, 129–31, 133, 141, 150
Reformation, 55, 59, 156, 168
Reines, Fred, 126
retribution, 84
rights, 19, 22, 39, 118, 164
*Roe v. Wade*, 83
Roman law, 2
Rota, Gian Carlo, 145
Rousseau, Jean-Jacques, 156, 163–65
Royce, Josiah, 139, 149–50
Rule of St. Benedict, 5
*Rules of Sociological Method* (Durkheim), 15

Russel, Bertrand, 101, 163
Russia, 46–48, 75–79, 119
Ryle, Gilbert, 104, 128

## S

Saint Louis Hegelians, 150
Saint Simon, Henri de, 17
Santayana, George, 2–3, 139, 159
*Santidad de revolución, La* ["The Sanctity of Revolution"] (Cardenal), 177–78
Sartre, Jean-Paul, 12, 42
Sayers, Dorothy, 180–81
Scheler, Max, 96
Schiller, Friedrich, 97
Scholasticism, 55, 115, 132
schools, 114. *See also* education
Schopenhauer, Arthur, 149
Schuhl, Pierre-Maxime, 5, 112
science: abstraction and, 147–48; in Ben-Menahem, 101–4; in Brague, 96–97, 143–44; in Durkheim, 15; in Farrington, 112–13; Freud and, 12–13; humanity and, 96; in Maimonides, 62, 64; philosophy and, 123–37; in Siedentop, 27; in Whitehead, 3–4, 110–11
*Science and the Modern World* (Whitehead), 3–4, 110
Scott, John T., 163–65
Seaton, Paul, 95, 167–68
Secada, Jorge, 142
Second Vatican Council. *See* Vatican II
sectionalism, 33
secularism, 31–32

secularization, 1, 16, 51
Semi-Pelagianism, 172
Seneca, 106
*Sentences* (Lombard), 105
Shklar, Judith, 163
Siedentop, Larry, 27–32
slavery, 39, 59, 78
Smith, Adam, 16
social contract, 164–65
*Social Contract, The* (Rousseau), 164
socialism, 27, 78, 149, 158–62, 177
Solzhenitsyn, Aleksandr, 75–78
*Solzhenitsyn: The Historical-Spiritual Destinies of Russia and the West* (Congdon), 75
Spaemann, Robert, 99
Spain, 78
Spengler, Oswald, 2
*Spirit of Laws* (Montesquieu), 52
stability, 102–3
state, 20, 33–34, 59. *See also* law
statistical mechanics, 103–4
Stein, Edith, 146–47
Stoics, 6, 18, 113
Strauss, David Fredrich, 150
Strauss, Leo, 69
*Successful Error, The* (Allers), 7, 11
*Suicide* (Durkheim), 15
Syria, 120

## T

Ten Commandments, 180–81
theocracy, 87–88
thermodynamics, 103–4
*Thought* (journal), 71–73
*Three Reformers* (Maritain), 163

"To the Christian Nobility" (Luther), 58
Toynbee, Arnold, 45
Trinity, 81

## U
Ukraine, 119–20
*Unintended Reformation, The* (Gregory), 55
United States, 89–90; Christianity and, 6–7, 22; cultural identity and, 2–3; law in, 81–84; liberalism and, 119–20; in Lippmann, 161–62; Puritans in, 87–89; Putin and, 46–47; Ukraine and, 120
Urban II, Pope, 30

## V
Valéry, Paul, 2
Vatican II, 39
Virginia Declaration of Rights, 89
Voltaire, 51–52, 156
von Hildebrand, Dietrich, 71

## W
Washington, George, 33–36
Watson, James, 124
Waugh, Evelyn, 20–21
*Wealth of Nations, The* (Smith), 16
White, Lynn, Jr., 4–5, 111–13
Whitehead, Alfred North, 2–5, 110, 113, 115
*Whose Justice, Which Rationality?* (MacIntyre), 82
Williams, Roger, 88
Wilson, Woodrow, 34
*Winds of Doctrine, The* (Santayana), 159
*World and the Individual, The* (Harris), 149

www.ingramcontent.com/pod-product-compliance
Lightning Source LLC
Chambersburg PA
CBHW030255010526
44107CB00053B/1718